Office 2016

Also covers Office 365

In easy steps is an imprint of In Easy Steps Limited
16 Hamilton Terrace · Holly Walk · Leamington Spa
Warwickshire · United Kingdom · CV32 4LY
www.ineasysteps.com

Notice of Liability
Every effort has been made to ensure that this book contains accurate
and current information. However, In Easy Steps Limited and the
author shall not be liable for any loss or damage suffered by readers
as a result of any information contained herein.

Trademarks
Microsoft® and Windows® are registered trademarks of Microsoft
Corporation. All other trademarks are acknowledged as belonging to
their respective companies.

In Easy Steps Limited supports The Forest Stewardship Council (FSC),
the leading international forest certification organization. All our titles
that are printed on Greenpeace approved FSC certified paper carry the
FSC logo.

MIX
Paper from
responsible sources
FSC® C020837

Printed and bound in the United Kingdom

ISBN 978-1-84078-650-7

Contents

4 Calculations   67

5 Manage Data   85

6 Presentations   107

1 Introducing Office 2016

This chapter discusses the latest version of Microsoft Office, with its ribbon style user interface. It identifies the range of editions, and outlines the requirements for installation. Also covered are: the process of starting applications, features used by all Office applications such as Preview and Save, Office document types, and compatibility with the older versions of applications.

Microsoft Office 2016

Microsoft Office is a suite of productivity applications that share common features and approaches. There have been many versions, but the latest version, released in September 2015, is Office 2016.

There are various "Office 2016" retail editions:

Office Home & Student 2016 edition contains:

- **Excel 2016**   Spreadsheet and data manager
- **PowerPoint 2016**   Presentations and slide shows
- **OneNote 2016**   For taking and collating notes
- **Word 2016**   Text editor and word processor

Office Home & Business 2016 edition contains all of the apps in the Home & Student edition, plus:

- **Outlook 2016**   Electronic mail and calendar

Office Professional 2016 edition contains all applications found in the Home & Business edition, plus two additional apps:

- **Access 2016**   Database manager
- **Publisher 2016**   Professional document creation

There are also various "Office 365" subscription editions:

Office 365 Personal edition contains all the apps (Excel, PowerPoint, OneNote, Word, Outlook, Access and Publisher) for one individual – licensed for 1 PC, 1 tablet, and 1 phone.

Office 365 Home edition also contains all the apps, but for an entire household – licensed for 5 PCs, 5 tablets, and 5 phones.

Office 365 Business edition contains all apps except Access, plus:

- **OneDrive for Business**   Online file storage and sharing

Office 365 Business Premium edition contains all the apps found in Office 365 Business (including OneDrive), plus three additional apps:

- **Microsoft Exchange**   Hosted messaging solution
- **SharePoint Online**   Collaboration web services
- **Skype for Business**   Hosted communications service

Office 365 Enterprise editions contain all applications found in the Office 365 Business Premium edition but provide additional security and information management tools.

There are estimated to be over 1.2 Billion users of Microsoft Office.

Office Online provides free web-based versions of the common apps, and Office Education provides extra special features for schools, teachers, and students.

In this book, the New icon pictured above is used to highlight new or enhanced features in Office 2016.

Ribbon Technology

Whichever edition of Office 2016 or Office 365 that you have, the applications they provide will all feature the graphical user interface based on the Ribbon. This replaced the menus and toolbars that were the essence of earlier versions of Office.

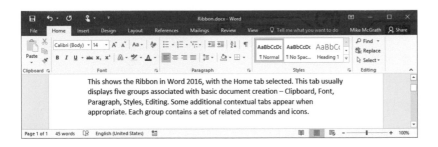

This shows the Ribbon in Word 2016, with the Home tab selected. This tab usually displays five groups associated with basic document creation – Clipboard, Font, Paragraph, Styles, Editing. Some additional contextual tabs appear when appropriate. Each group contains a set of related commands and icons.

The Ribbon contains command buttons and icons, organized in a set of tabs, each containing groups of commands associated with specific functions. The purpose is to make the relevant features more intuitive, and more readily available. This allows you to concentrate on the tasks you want to perform, rather than the details of how you will carry out the activities. Some tabs appear only when certain objects are selected. These are known as "contextual" tabs, and provide functions that are specific to the selected object. For example, when you select an inserted image, the **Picture Tools**, **Format** tab and its command groups are displayed.

This shows the Picture Tools Format group, which is added to the Home tab in Word 2016 when you select a picture that has been inserted into the document.

The Ribbon interface also provides extended ScreenTips that can contain text, images, and links to more help. The tips display as you move the mouse pointer over an option, and describe the functions or give keyboard shortcuts.

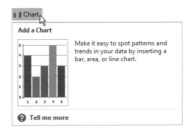

Hot tip

This result-oriented user interface was first introduced in Office 2007, and now appears in all the applications in Office 2016.

NEW

For systems with touch-enabled monitors, Office 2016 offers a **Touch Mode** ribbon with larger and more widely spaced icons (see page 14).

What's Needed

To use Microsoft Office 2016, you will need at least the following components in your computer:

- 1GHz processor (32-bit or 64-bit)

- 2GB RAM memory

- 3GB available disk space

- 1280 × 800 or larger resolution monitor

- DirectX 10 graphics card

- Windows 10, 8/8.1, 7 SP1, or Windows Server 10, 2012 R2, 2012, 2008 R2

Beware

These are the minimum requirements. A higher-speed processor, with additional memory will produce faster results.

Some functions will have additional requirements, for example:

- Touch-enabled monitor for controlling the system

- Internet connection for online help

- CD-ROM or DVD drive for install, backup and data storage

If your computer is running Windows 8, 8.1 or 10, the system specifications will meet or exceed requirements for Office 2016.

Don't forget

These system properties are for the PC used in this book, which is running Windows 10 Pro. However, the tasks and topics covered will generally apply to any supported operating system environment.

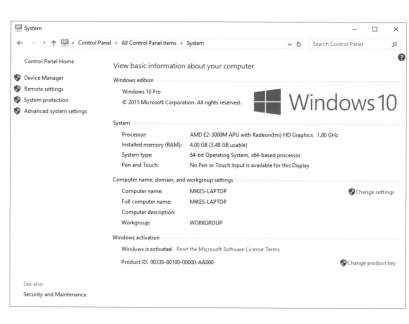

Installing Office 2016

You can buy your preferred version of Microsoft Office 2016 in disk format from a retail source or download it directly from Microsoft. Windows 10 provides a default "Get Office" item on the Start menu that launches your web browser at the Office download page **products.office.com**. Here, you can select one of the Office 365 subscription-based versions of Microsoft Office 2016. These provide fully installed Office apps that work across multiple devices and are continuously upgraded – so are always up to date. For example, you might choose the Office 365 Personal version, which lets you use Office on one PC, one tablet, and one phone. This also gives you a massive 1TB of storage for one user.

To compare the various versions of Office visit **products.office.com/ en-us/buy/compare- microsoft-office- products**

1 Click the **Get Office** tile or Start menu item – to launch your web browser

2 Select your version then enter the purchase details – to begin installation

Get Office

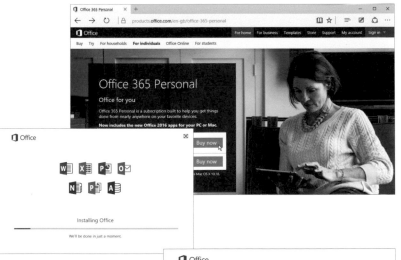

Hot tip

Microsoft is eager to encourage adoption of the subscription versions – Office 365 Personal edition also includes 60 minutes per month of Skype calls to cellphones and landlines.

3 Take a break until the Office completion dialog appears

Start an Application

With Microsoft Office 2016 installed under Windows 10, you have a number of ways to launch the Office apps:

1 The installation of Office should have added colored icons for various Office apps onto the Windows Desktop taskbar. Click the blue 'W' icon to launch the Word 2016 app

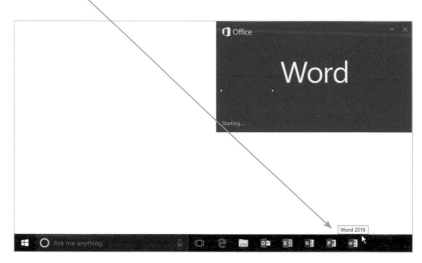

2 In either Desktop or Tablet mode, click or tap the Start button, then choose **All apps**

3 Now, scroll down the A-Z list to the **W** category heading

4 Choose the **Word 2016** item to launch the Word 2016 app

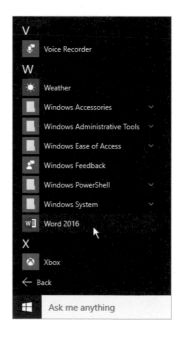

5 In the taskbar Search box, type "word" to search for the Word app on your system

6 Now, click or tap the **Word 2016** item from the search results to launch the Word 2016 app

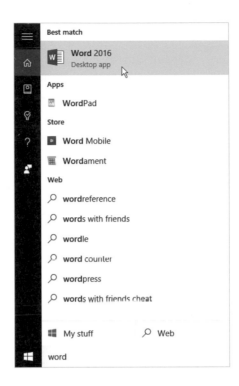

You can right-click the Word 2016 item on the **All apps** list, and select **Pin to Start** to add a tile to the Tablet mode Start screen and Desktop mode Start group.

7 Say "Hey Cortana" into your system microphone to wake up your Personal Digital Assistant

8 Now say "start Word" into the microphone to launch the Word 2016 app

Cortana is new in Windows 10 but performance may vary by region. If Cortana is not working or enabled in your country, try setting your region to "United States" in **Settings**, **Time & language**, **Region & language**.

Application Start

Document-based Office applications open at the Start screen with the **Recent** list and various document templates.

The Touch/Mouse Mode button appears by default when you have a touch-enabled monitor. To add it if not displayed, click the Customize Quick Access Toolbar button and then select Touch/Mouse Mode. You can then display the enlarged Ribbon on a standard monitor.

1 Select an Office 2016 application item such as Word, using any of the methods described on the previous pages, to display that application's Start screen

2 Select **Blank document** to begin a new editing session

3 Click the Touch/Mouse Mode button on the Quick Access Toolbar, and then select **Touch**

4 The expanded Ribbon is displayed

The Application Window

When you start an Office application such as Excel, PowerPoint or Word, the program window is displayed with a blank document named "Book1", "Presentation1", or "Document1" respectively. Using Word for example, parts of the application window include:

Backstage (File tab) Quick Access Toolbar Document name Tabs

"Tell Me" Help box
Ribbon Display options

Minimize/Restore/Close

Ribbon Command icons (display lists or galleries)

Collapse the Ribbon

Group launch button (shows dialog box)

Vertical scroll area

Status bar Horizontal scroll area View buttons Zoom level

When you have updated your document and want to save your progress so far, click **File** to display the Backstage command screen and then select **Save** to name and save the document. You can save it in your OneDrive (see page 16) or on your computer.

File commands Save locations Browse the selected location Recent Folders

The **Tell Me** Help box is new in Office 2016 and is available in Word, Excel, Outlook and PowerPoint.

Don't forget

From Backstage you can select **Info** for details about your document, or **New** to start another document, or **Open** to display an existing document. There are also printing and sharing options provided.

Your OneDrive

To save documents to your OneDrive online storage:

1 Select **File**, **Save As**, then click the OneDrive button

OneDrive was previously known as SkyDrive. When you set up a Microsoft Account to sign in to Windows, you are assigned an allowance of up to 15GB online storage which is managed on the Microsoft OneDrive server (see also page 222). An Office 365 subscription gives you a further 1TB of storage *(correct at the time of printing)*.

2 Confirm or amend the document name then choose the appropriate folder, e.g. Documents

3 Click **Save** to upload the document and save it to your OneDrive folder

4 To access your OneDrive from a browser, go online to **onedrive.live.com**, and sign in if prompted

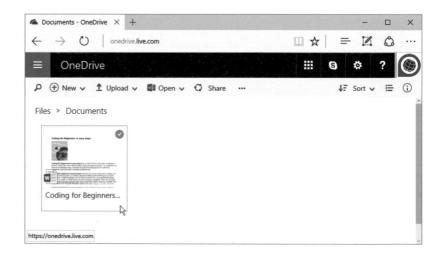

OneDrive lets you access and edit your documents from any computer where you sign in with the same Microsoft Account. You can also access your OneDrive and documents from a web browser.

...cont'd

If you are running Windows 7 or 8, you can download OneDrive for Windows to store your Office 2016 documents. You can also download OneDrive for other operating systems, such as Android, to allow ready access to your documents across all your devices.

OneDrive comes pre-installed on Windows 10.

1   Launch your web browser and navigate to the OneDrive home page at **onedrive.live.com** and click **Download**

2   Select the operating system you require – for example, choose **Windows** if you are running Windows 7 or 8

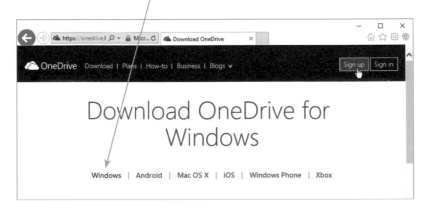

After installation you'll be offered the option to sync all of your files and folders on OneDrive, or choose selected folders to sync.

3   Click the **Sign in** button, if you already have a Microsoft Account, or click the **Sign up** button to create an account

4   The application is downloaded and installed, and the OneDrive is created where you can save your documents

Live Preview

With the Ribbon interface, you can immediately see the full effect of format options, such as fonts and styles, on your document by simply pointing to the proposed change. For example, to see font formatting changes:

1 Highlight the text that you may wish to change, then select the **Home** tab

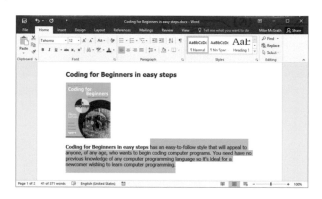

In earlier versions, you would be shown a preview of the new font or style using a small amount of sample text. Office 2016 displays full previews.

18

2 Click the arrow next to the **Font** box and move the mouse pointer over the fonts you'd like to preview

The selected text is temporarily altered to show the font (or the font size, color or highlight) you point to.

3 Click the font you want to apply to the text, or press **Esc** to close the options

4 Similarly, you can preview Text Effects, Highlight Colors and Font Colors

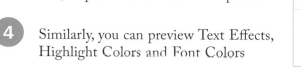

Working with the Ribbon

The Ribbon takes up a significant amount of the window space, especially when you have a lower-resolution display. To hide it:

1 Click the **Collapse the Ribbon** button (see page 15), or

Right-click the tab bar and select **Collapse the Ribbon**

2 The Quick Access Toolbar and the Tab bar will still be displayed while the Ribbon is minimized

3 The Ribbon reappears temporarily when you click one of the tabs, so you can select the required command

4 Alternatively, press and release the **Alt** key to display keyboard shortcuts for the tabs

5 Press **Alt** + *shortcut key*, for example **Alt** + **H** to select Home and display the Ribbon and shortcuts for that tab

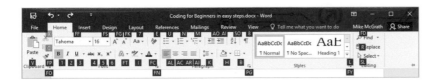

Hot tip

You can also select **Ribbon Display Options** on the Windows Titlebar and choose **Show Tabs** to hide the Ribbon, or **Show Tabs and Commands** to reveal the Ribbon.

19

Don't forget

Hold down the **Alt** key and press the keys in sequence for a two-letter shortcut, such as **Alt** + **FS** (Font Size), and press **Esc** to go back up a level.

Quick Access Toolbar

The Quick Access Toolbar contains a set of commands that are independent of the selected tab. There are five buttons initially:

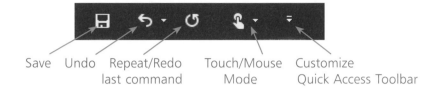

Save   Undo   Repeat/Redo   Touch/Mouse   Customize
                last command   Mode   Quick Access Toolbar

Hot tip

You can right-click any command on the Ribbon and select **Add to Quick Access Toolbar**.

Add to Quick Access Toolbar
Customize Quick Access Toolbar...
Show Quick Access Toolbar Below the Ribbon
Customize the Ribbon...
Collapse the Ribbon

1 Click the **Save** button to save the current contents of the document to your OneDrive, or to the drive on your PC

2 Click **Repeat** to carry out the last action again, or click **Undo** to reverse the last action, and click again to reverse the previous actions in turn

Hot tip

The **Save As** dialog will open the first time you press the **Save** button for a new document.

3 When you have pressed **Undo**, the **Repeat** button changes to become the **Redo** button, which will re-apply in turn the actions that you have reversed

4 Click the **Customize** button to add or remove icons, using the shortlist of frequently-referenced commands

Customize Quick Access Toolbar
New
Open
✓ Save
Email
Quick Print
Print Preview and Print
Spelling & Grammar
✓ Undo
✓ Redo
Draw Table
✓ Touch/Mouse Mode
More Commands...
Show Below the Ribbon

Don't forget

You can also click the **File** tab, then select the application **Options** and select **Quick Access Toolbar** to display this dialog box.

5 Click **More Commands...** to display the full list of commands, then add and remove entries as desired

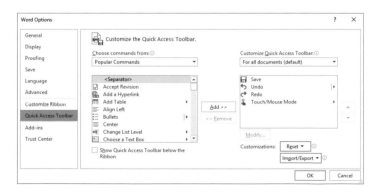

Office Document Types

The files you create using the Office applications will be office documents of various types, including:

- **Word document**   Formatted text and graphics
- **Publisher publication** Flyers and brochures
- **Excel worksheet**   Spreadsheets and data lists
- **PowerPoint presentation** Presentations and slide shows

Each item will be a separate file. Typically, these may be saved in your OneDrive Documents folder (or locally on your computer).

1 To review your files, open File Explorer and select your OneDrive Documents folder

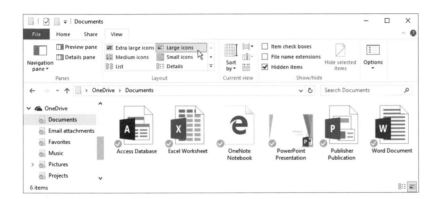

You can specify another folder or sub-folder to organize particular sets of documents.

2 This shows the files as large icons. For other styles, click the **View** tab and select, for example, **Details**, to show the file information including date modified, size, and type

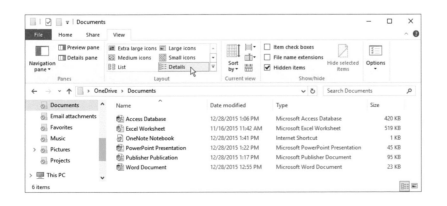

In some applications, groups of related items are stored together in a specially structured file, for example, data tables, queries, and reports in an Access database.

File Extensions

To see the file extensions that are associated with the various document types:

1 In File Explorer, select the **View** tab and in the **Show/Hide** section of the Ribbon click the box labeled **File name extensions**

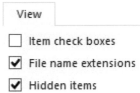

You can also change File Explorer Options in the Control Panel, under **Appearance and Personalization**.

File Explorer Options

2 View the contents of your library folder

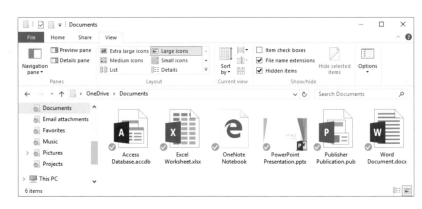

3 The file type will be shown, along with the file name, whichever folder view you choose

Files saved in Office 2016 use OpenXML formats and extensions, for example **.docx** and **.xlsx**. Older Office files will have file types such as **.doc** and **.xls**.

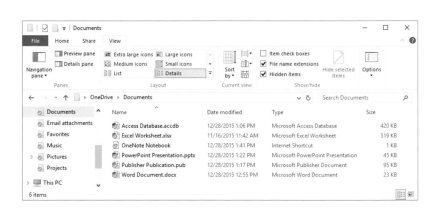

Compatibility Mode

Office 2016 will open documents created in previous versions of Office applications, for example **.doc** (Word) or **.xls** (Excel).

1 Click the **File** tab and select **Open**, then click the down arrow for the list of document types supported

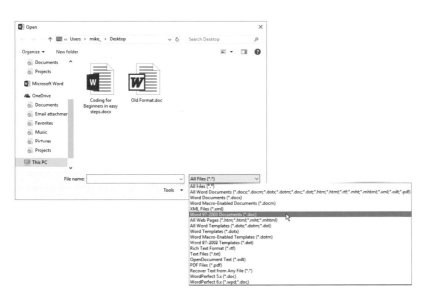

You may need to save documents in Compatibility Mode, as some users you wish to share files with may not have Office 2016.

2 Choose the document type, "Word 97-2003" for example, then select the specific name, e.g. **Old Format.doc**

Compatibility Mode prevents the use of new or enhanced features, so the documents can continue to be used by systems with older versions of the applications.

3 Documents created in previous versions (including **.docx** files from Word 2010) are opened in Compatibility Mode

Convert to Office 2016

If you have opened a document in Compatibility Mode, you can convert it to the standard Office 2016 format.

Hot tip

You can also click the **File** tab, select **Save As**, and choose the standard Office format (e.g. Word Document) to carry out the conversion.

Beware

Converting will create a file of the same name, but with the new Office 2016 format extension. The original file will be deleted.

Don't forget

With **Save As**, you have the option to change the file name, and the location for the new document.

1 Select the **File** tab and **Info**, then the **Convert** button

2 Click **OK** to confirm, and the file type will be amended

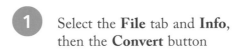

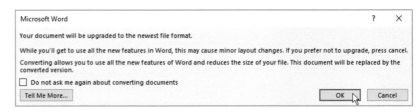

3 To replace the original file, select **File** and then **Save** – see the file extension change in the Word title bar to the new **.docx** file type

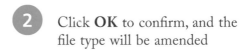

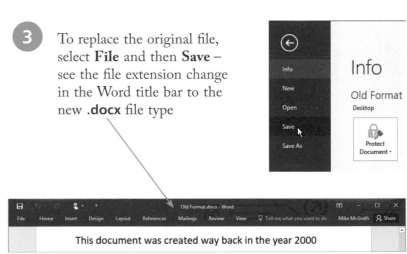

This document was created way back in the year 2000

4 To retain the original while creating a new file in Office 2016 format, select **File**, **Save As**, then click **Save**

2 Create Word Documents

This covers the basics of word processing, using the Word application in Office 2016. It covers entering, selecting and copying text, saving and autosaving, and proofing the text. It looks at the use of styles to structure the document, and adding document features such as pictures, columns, and word counts. It also discusses ways of creating tables, the use of Paste Special, and the facilities for printing.

Create a Word Document

There are several ways to create a Word document:

1 Right-click any empty space on the Desktop and select **New, Microsoft Word Document** from the context menu that appears

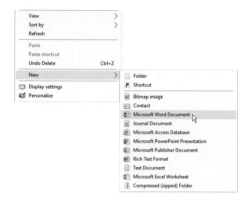

A new right-click document, as shown in Step 1, will be named **New Microsoft Word Document**, though you can rename this to be more relevant by right-clicking on the title and overtyping it. It will appear as an icon on the Desktop.

2 Start Word and select **Blank document** (see page 14) to create a document temporarily named "Document1"

Double-click the file icon to open the document.

3 If Word is open, select the **File** tab, click **New**, and choose **Blank document** to create another document

Enter Text

1 Click on the page and type the text that you want. If the text is longer than a single line, Word automatically starts the new line for you

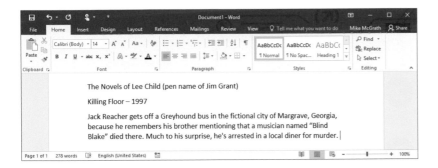

The Novels of Lee Child (pen name of Jim Grant)

Killing Floor – 1997

Jack Reacher gets off a Greyhound bus in the fictional city of Margrave, Georgia, because he remembers his brother mentioning that a musician named "Blind Blake" died there. Much to his surprise, he's arrested in a local diner for murder.

2 Press **Enter** when you need to insert a blank line or start a new paragraph

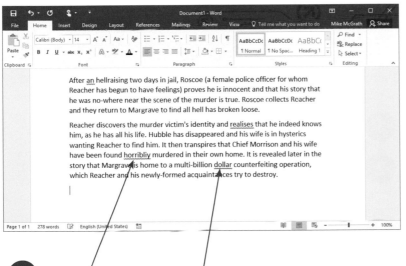

After an hellraising two days in jail, Roscoe (a female police officer for whom Reacher has begun to have feelings) proves he is innocent and that his story that he was no-where near the scene of the murder is true. Roscoe collects Reacher and they return to Margrave to find all hell has broken loose.

Reacher discovers the murder victim's identity and realises that he indeed knows him, as he has all his life. Hubble has disappeared and his wife is in hysterics wanting Reacher to find him. It then transpires that Chief Morrison and his wife have been found horribly murdered in their own home. It is revealed later in the story that Margrave is home to a multi-billion dollar counterfeiting operation, which Reacher and his newly-formed acquaintances try to destroy.

3 Red (spelling) or Blue (grammar and style) wavy underlines may appear – to indicate "proofing errors"

4 Click the ⌨ button on the status bar to correct them one by one, or correct them all at the same time, when you've finished typing the whole document (see page 31)

You can copy and paste text from other sources, such as web pages. Use **Paste Options** (see page 29) to avoid copying styles and formats along with the text.

You may see blue wavy underscores to indicate contextual spelling errors (misused words), such as "Their" in place of "There".

Select the **Tell Me** box to see a **Recently Used** drop-down list appear showing the last five commands you used.

Select and Copy Text

In Word, there are numerous ways to select the portion of text you require, using the mouse or the keyboard, as preferred. To select the entire document, use one of these options:

1 Select the **Home** tab, click **Select** in the Editing group, and then click the **Select All** command

2 Move the mouse pointer to the left of any text until it turns into a right–pointing arrow, then triple-click

3 Press the shortcut keys **Ctrl** + **A** to select all of the text

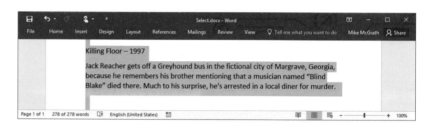

There are many mouse and keyboard options for selecting a piece of text in the body of the document. For example:

1 Double-click anywhere in a word to select it

2 Hold down **Ctrl** and click anywhere in a sentence to select the whole sentence

3 To select a portion of text, click at the start, hold down the left mouse button and drag the pointer over the text, then release the button when the required text is selected

...cont'd

You can use text selection in combination with the Clipboard tools, to copy or move multiple pieces of text in the same operation. For example:

1 Select the first section of required text using the mouse to highlight it

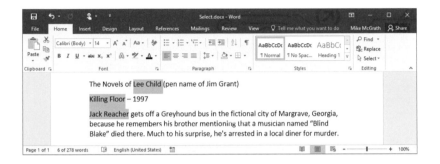

2 Hold down the **Ctrl** key and select additional pieces of text

3 Select **Home** and click the **Copy** button in the Clipboard group

4 Click the position in the document where the text is required, then select **Home** and click the **Paste** button

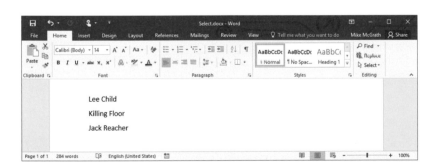

5 If you've copied several pieces of text, each piece appears on a separate line, so you will need to delete the end-of-line characters to join them up

You can use the keyboard shortcuts **Ctrl + C** (copy), **Ctrl + X** (cut), and **Ctrl + V** (paste) instead of the Clipboard buttons, as well as right-clicking and selecting options from the context menu.

Hot tip

Click the **Cut** button if you want to move the text rather than copy it.

Click the arrow below the **Paste** button, then click **Paste Options** and choose between **Keep Source Formatting**, **Merge Formatting**, and **Keep Text Only**.

Save the Document

When you are building a document, Word will periodically save a copy of the document, just in case a problem arises. This minimizes the amount of text you may need to re-enter if a document is lost, accidentally deleted or becomes corrupt. This feature is known as "AutoRecover". To check the settings:

1 Click the **File** tab, select **Options**, then the **Save** command

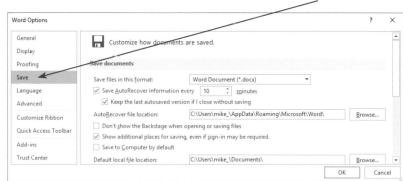

If the system terminates abnormally, any data entered since the last AutoRecover operation will be lost.

By default, Word will save AutoRecover information every ten minutes, but you can change the frequency using the settings in the Word Options screen above.

To make an immediate save of your document:

1 Click the **Save** button on the Quick Access Toolbar

2 The first time, you'll be prompted to confirm the location, the file name, and the document type that you want to use

You can also select **File**, **Save As**, to specify a new location, name, or document type.

3 On subsequent saves, the document on the hard disk will be updated immediately, without further interaction

Correct Proofing Errors

When you've entered all the text, you can correct proofing errors.

1 Press **Ctrl + Home** to go to the start of the document, select the **Review** tab, then choose **Spelling & Grammar**

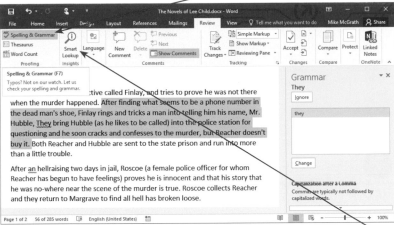

The **Spelling & Grammar** check will begin from the current typing cursor location unless you move it to the start of the document. Ensure that the appropriate language dictionary is enabled!

2 The first proofing error is found – a Grammar error. Click the **Change** button to accept the offered suggestion, or click the **Ignore** button to decline the suggestion

Now in Office 2016 you can use **Smart Lookup** to find a definition or description of the highlighted text.

3 The next proofing error is found – a Spelling error. Click the **Change** button or **Ignore** button as preferred, or
Click the **Change All** button or **Ignore All** button to correct all occurrences in the document

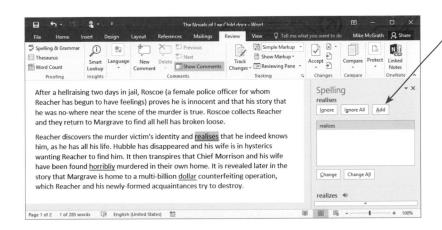

Use the **Add** button to add an error-raising word to the dictionary if it is likely to occur often in your documents – so it will no longer be reported as an error.

Change Proofing Settings

1 Select the **File** tab, then **Word Options** and **Proofing**

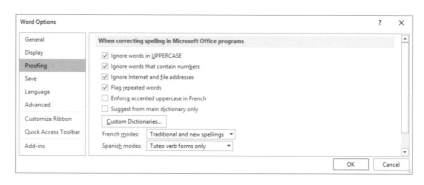

You can make changes to the settings for the spelling checks, and also for the grammar and style checks.

2 Some settings, such as **Ignore words in UPPERCASE** and **Flag repeated words**, apply to all Office applications

If you'd rather not use the grammar checker, clear the boxes for **Mark grammar errors as you type** and **Check grammar with spelling**. Alternatively, you can hide errors in that particular document.

3 Some proofing options are specific to the particular Office application, e.g. Word's **Mark grammar errors as you type**

4 Some options are specific to the document being worked on

5 The spell checker in Word is contextual, identifying words that are spelled correctly but used inappropriately, and suggesting more suitable alternatives

Apply Styles

33

1 Select the **Home** tab, then click in the main heading and select the style for **Heading 1** for major emphasis

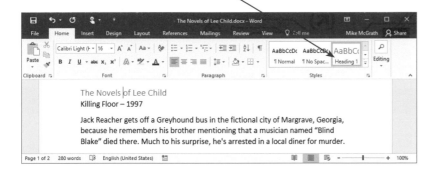

You can change the style for parts of the text to suit the particular contents, using the Styles group on the **Home** tab.

2 Click inside one of the subsidiary headings and select the style for **Heading 2** for minor emphasis

Click the down-arrow to show the next row of styles, or click the group dialog launcher button to see more styles.

3 Click within one of the text paragraphs and select the style for **No Spacing** to condense the paragraph

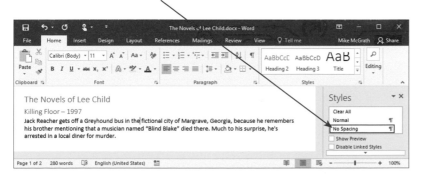

Apply these two styles to other headings and paragraphs. To repeat a style, select an example, double-click the Format Painter icon, and then click each similar item in turn.

Outline View

When you have structured the document using headings, you can view it as an outline:

1 Select the **View** tab and click the **Outline** button, to switch to Outline view and enable the **Outlining** tab

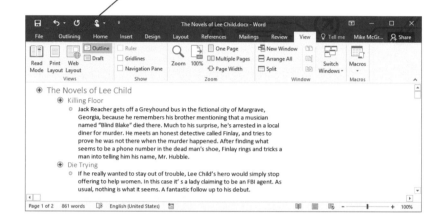

2 In the **Outlining** tab's Outline Tools group, click the box labeled **Show First Line Only** to see more entries

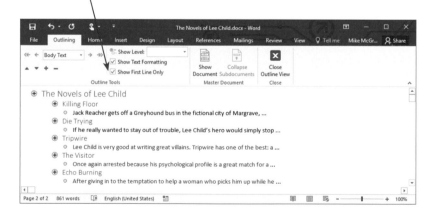

This makes it easier for you to review the whole document. You might decide that you want to try a different sequence, for example, in a chronological order of events rather than the date of publication. Outline view makes it easy to reposition the entries.

1 Click the arrow next to **Show Level**, and choose "Level 2"

2 Click the **+** button beside an item to select it. For example, click to select "The Enemy" item

This will display the selected level, and all the higher levels in the Outline of the document.

You can click the **+** button beside an entry to select it, and then drag it to the required location.

35

3 Now, click the ▲ Up arrow button in the Outline Tools group, and the selected entry, with all its subsidiary levels and text, will move one row for each click on the button

The Outline Tools group also provides buttons that allow you to promote or demote selected entries.

4 Repeat to reposition another entry, e.g. "Tripwire"

5 Select an item then click the ▼ down-arrow in the Outline Tools group to move an entry lower in the list

Insert a Picture

1 Position the typing cursor at the location where you want to add a picture, inserting a blank line if desired

2 Select the **Insert** tab and click the appropriate icon or command, e.g. **Picture** (in the Illustrations group)

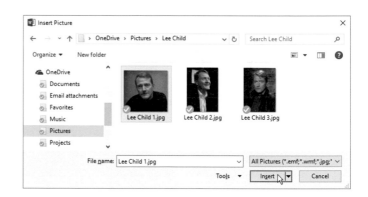

3 Locate the file for the picture, and click the **Insert** button

You can adjust the position of the picture on the page of text.

1 Click the **Position** button in the **Format** tab's Arrange group and move the mouse pointer over the buttons

The **Format** tab allows you to change the size, select a frame, and adjust the brightness, contrast, and color of the picture.

2 A live preview will be displayed. Click the appropriate button for the position you prefer

3 Click the up or down arrow on the height, to adjust the size of the picture – see that the width automatically gets changed in proportion to the adjusted height you choose

The original proportions of the picture will be maintained, when you make changes to the height or width.

Hot tip

Having chosen the layout, you can select the picture to drag it and make fine adjustments.

Page Layout

The **Layout** tab allows you to control how the document contents are placed on the page, by just clicking one of the function command buttons in the Page Setup group.

To display the vertical and horizontal rulers, as shown here, select the **View** tab and then click the **Ruler** box, from the Show group.

1 Click the **Orientation** button to select **Portrait** or **Landscape**

2 Click the **Size** button to select the paper size from the list, or click **More Paper Sizes...** to show other choices, including **Custom Size**

You can also press the arrowed group button in the Page Setup group to display the **Page Setup** dialog.

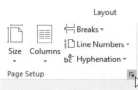

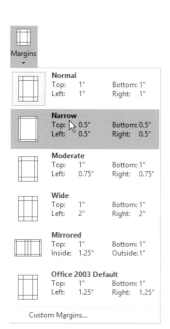

3 Click the **Margins** button to choose one of the predefined setups, e.g. **Narrow**, or click **Custom Margins...** to display the **Page Setup** dialog, and then enter the specific values

Display in Columns

1 Select the text to put into columns and click the **Layout** tab, then select **Columns** from the Page Setup group

Leave all of the text unselected if you wish to apply the columns to the whole document.

2 Choose the number of columns required, e.g. **Three**

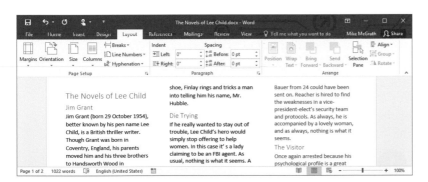

3 Click in the body text, select the **Home** tab, click **Select**, **Select Text with Similar Formatting**, and click the **Justify** button

Choose **Justify** for the paragraph text, to help give the document the appearance of newspaper columns. Choose **Center** for the title text, to place it over the three columns.

Word Count

If you are preparing a document for a publication, such as a club magazine, you may need to keep track of the number of words:

Don't forget

When there is text selected, the status bar shows word counts for the selection and the whole document.

Page 1 of 2   5 of 1022 words

1 View the word count for the document on the status bar

2 Click the word count to display the detailed counts for pages, paragraphs, lines, and characters

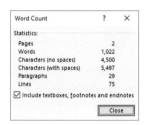

For a fuller analysis of the contents of the document:

Hot tip

You can also display the word count details by selecting the **Review** tab and clicking the **Word Count** button in the Proofing group.

1 Select **File**, **Options**, **Proofing**, then **Show readability statistics**

2 Select the **Review** tab, then click the **Spelling & Grammar** button in the Proofing group and check the document

3 After the spelling check is completed, the document statistics are displayed

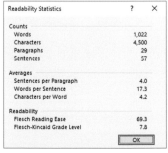

Create a Table

To create a table in your document:

You'll see previews in the document of the indicated table sizes as you move the pointer across the **Insert Table** area.

1 Click the point where you want to add the table, then click the **Insert** tab, and select **Table**

2 Select the desired number of rows and columns, then click to insert the table and type in the contents

Press the **Tab** key to move across columns, or use the arrow keys to navigate around the table. Click and drag a separator line to adjust the width of a column.

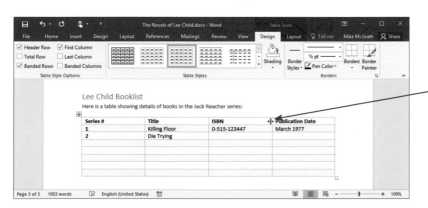

Convert Text to Table

If you already have the text that's needed for the table, perhaps taken from another document, you can convert the text into a table:

1 Make sure that the cell entries are separated by a comma or tab mark, or some other unique character

The cursor must be in the table area to display the **Table Tools** tab. Select its **Layout** tab to see operations such as insert, delete, and align.

Select **AutoFit to contents**, to adjust the column widths to match the data in those cells.

2 Highlight the text, select the **Insert** tab, and then click **Table**, **Convert Text to Table**

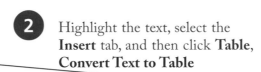

3 Specify your particular separation character and then click **OK**

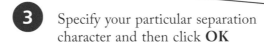

4 The table will be created with the data inserted into the relevant cells, which may be expanded to hold the data

Select **Home**, then click the **Show/Hide** button in the Paragraph group to display tabs and paragraph marks. Two consecutive commas or tabs indicate an empty cell. Paragraph marks separate the rows.

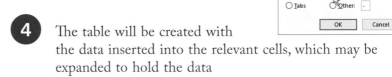

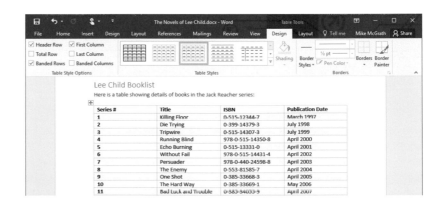

Lee Child Booklist
Here is a table showing details of books in the Jack Reacher series:

Series #	Title	ISBN	Publication Date
1	Killing Floor	0-515-12344-7	March 1997
2	Die Trying	0-399-14379-3	July 1998
3	Tripwire	0-515-14307-3	July 1999
4	Running Blind	978-0-515-14350-8	April 2000
5	Echo Burning	0-515-13331-0	April 2001
6	Without Fail	978-0-515-14431-4	April 2002
7	Persuader	978-0-440-24598-8	April 2003
8	The Enemy	0-553-81585-7	April 2004
9	One Shot	0-385-33668-3	April 2005
10	The Hard Way	0-385-33669-1	May 2006
11	Bad Luck and Trouble	0-385-34055-9	April 2007

Paste Special

To copy text without including its formatting and graphics:

1 Highlight the text you want, then right-click the selected area and click the **Copy** command

Information copied from other documents, or web pages, may include graphics, formatting, and colors inappropriate for your document.

2 Click in the document where the text is needed, and from the **Home** tab, click the arrow below the **Paste** button

Graphical information won't be copied, even if it has the appearance of text (as with the initial "A" for Andrew in text copied for this example).

3 Click **Paste Special** and choose **Paste, Unformatted Text**

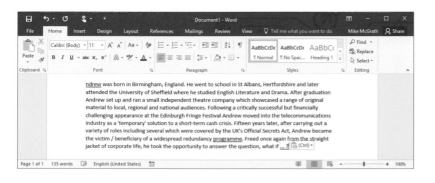

The copied text will inherit the format of that part of the document you clicked before carrying out the paste operation.

Print Document

1 To print your document from within Word, click the **File** tab and select **Print** (or press **Ctrl + P**)

In Office 2016 programs, you can preview and print your documents at one location – in the **Print** section of the Backstage area.

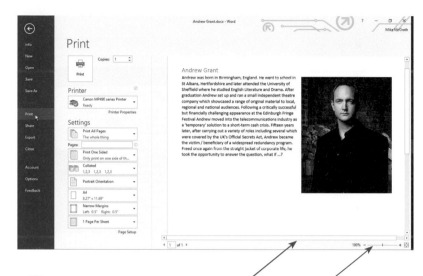

2 From here, you can use the scroll bars, the zoom slider, and the page change buttons to preview the document

You can view the document as it will appear in print by selecting the **View** tab and selecting the **Print Layout** button from the Views group.

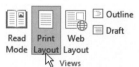

3 Select the specific printer to use

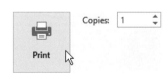
Canon MP490 series Printer
Ready

4 Choose the page/s to print

Print Current Page
Just this page

5 Adjust other settings, such as the paper and margin sizes

6 Specify the number of copies, then click the **Print** button

Copies: 1

Print

Quick Print

You can add the **Quick Print** button to the Quick Access Toolbar (see page 14), to get an immediate print of the current document, using the default settings.

3 Complex Documents

Microsoft Word can be used to create and edit more complex documents, such as booklets and brochures. This chapter covers importing text, inserting illustrations, creating tables of contents, and illustrations. It shows how templates can be used to help create documents, and also introduces Publisher, the Office application that is specifically designed for desktop publishing.

Start a Booklet

To illustrate some of the facilities available for creating and organizing complex documents, we'll go through the process of importing and structuring the text for a booklet. Our example uses the text for "A Study in Scarlet" by Sir Arthur Conan Doyle.

1. Start by typing the book title, author, and chapter names

Hot tip

The text for books in the public domain can be found online from websites such as Project Gutenberg at gutenberg.org

2. When you've entered all the chapter headings, set the language. This is a British book, so press **Ctrl + A** to highlight all text, select **Review**, **Language**, **Set Proofing Language**, **English (United Kingdom)** and click **OK**

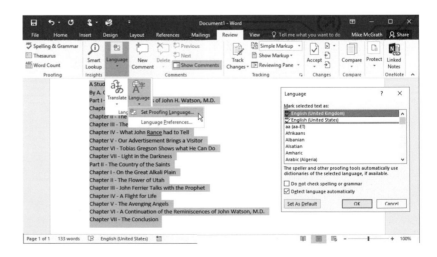

Beware

You need to highlight all the text to change to a different language for the whole document.

3. Click **Save** on the Quick Access Toolbar, and provide a name for the document, or accept the suggested name

Choose Page Arrangement

Now, specify the paper size, the margins and the page style:

1 Select the page **Layout** tab, and click **Size** to choose the paper size you are printing on, for example "Letter"

2 Click the group button on the Page Setup group to display the **Page Setup** dialog

3 In the **Pages** section, click the **Multiple pages** arrow button, then select **Book fold** from the drop-down menu

4 Click the **Sheets per booklet** arrow button, then select **4** from the drop-down menu

You can specify the number of sheets in multiples of 4 up to 40, to assemble the document in blocks of pages, or choose **All** to assemble the document as a single booklet.

Hot tip

Similarly, you can click **Margins** to select the size you want to use, for example "Normal".

Don't forget

The orientation changes to Landscape, and you get four pages of the document on each piece of paper (printed on both sides). A four-sheet booklet, for example, would be printed as:

Front   4 1

Back   2 3

Create the Structure

1 Highlight the text for the chapter titles

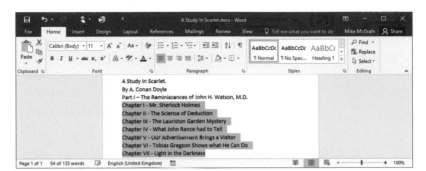

Don't forget

This particular book has two parts, with seven chapters in each part.

2 Click the **Home** tab and select **Styles**, **Heading 1**

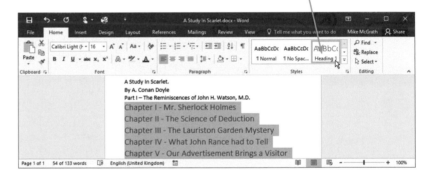

3 With the chapter titles still selected, click the **Center** button in the Paragraph group

Don't forget

The formatting changes center the chapter titles over the text that will be inserted (see page 50).

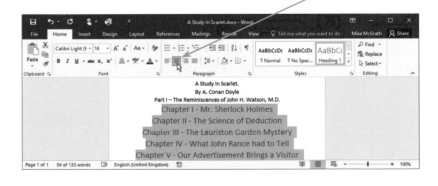

…**cont'd**

4 To replace hyphens with line breaks in the chapter titles, click the Editing group's **Replace** button, to open the **Find and Replace** dialog

5 In the **Find what** box, type a hyphen with a space either side, i.e. " - " (without the quotation marks)

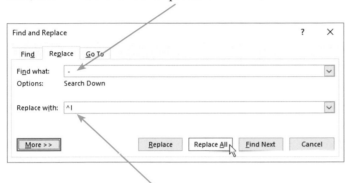

6 In the **Replace with** box, type the "^l" (carat, lowercase L) control code for a line break, then click **Replace All**

7 This changes all the occurrences in the selected text. Click **No** to skip the remainder of the document, to avoid changing hyphens elsewhere in the text

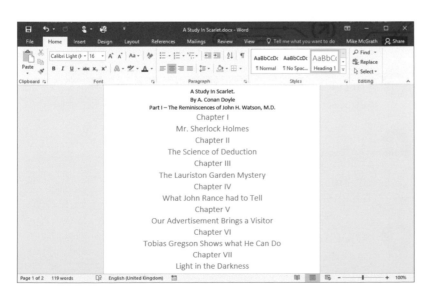

Hot tip

Steps 4 to 6 illustrate how you can use **Find** and **Replace** to insert special characters, such as line breaks. You can click the **More** button and select **Special**, **Manual Line Break** to insert the required code.

Don't forget

To see paragraph and line break codes, click the **Show/Hide** button (in the Paragraph group on the **Home** tab).

Chapter·I↵
Mr.·Sherlock·Holmes¶

Note that each title remains a single item, even though spread over two lines.

Import Text

1 Click immediately to the left of the "Chapter I" title, and select **Insert**, **Page Break**, to start the chapter on a new page

Type paragraphs of text, insert text from a file, or copy and paste text from a file if you just want part of the contents.

2 Click the page, just past the end of the title, and press **Enter** to add a new blank line in body text style

This option was known as **Insert File** in earlier versions of Word. It allows you to transfer the contents from various file types, including Word, web, and text.

3 In the Text group, select **Object**, and choose **Text from File**

4 Locate the folder and file holding the chapter text

5 Click **Insert** to add the text

6 Click **OK** to select the appropriate encoding, if prompted

The text will be copied to the document at the required location.

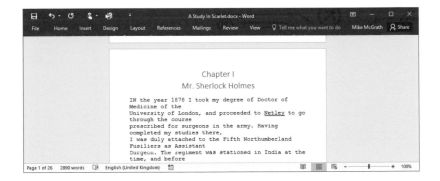

Step 6 is only required when the system needs your help in interpreting the imported text.

Repeat steps 1 to 5 for each chapter in the book.

To adjust the style for the inserted text:

1 Click anywhere in the inserted text, click the **Home** tab, then in the Editing group, click **Select** and choose **Select Text with Similar Formatting**

2 Select your preferred style, e.g. **Normal**, **No Spacing**, plus **Justify** and all of the inserted text will be converted

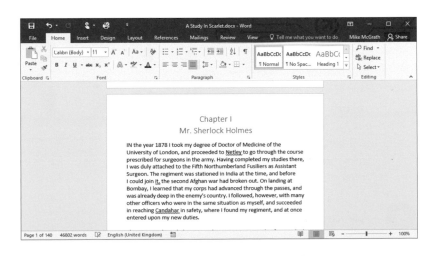

The inserted text may not have the format you require, but you can change all of the inserted text in a single operation, to a style that you prefer.

Insert Illustrations

1 Find the location for an illustration. For example, select **Home**, **Find**, and enter a search term, such as "Figure"

Hot tip

The sample text has the titles for the illustrations at the required locations, in the form of:
Figure: *Illustration title*

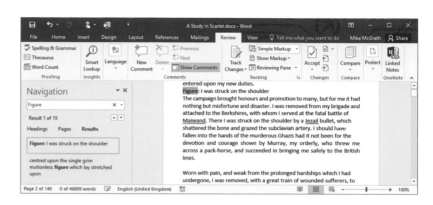

2 Select the placeholder text describing the illustration, then choose the **Insert** tab and click **Pictures**

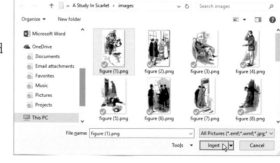

Don't forget

You can insert pictures from image files of all the usual types, including bitmap, JPEG (photos), and GIF (web graphics).

3 Locate the file containing the required illustration and click **Insert**, and the picture is inserted into the document, in line with the text

4 Adjust its size and position as required

Add Captions

Repeat the steps from these two pages to insert a picture and a caption for each of the figures in the book.

1 From the **References** tab, select **Insert Caption**

2 Click **OK** to accept the automatic number

If the document doesn't already contain the title for the illustration, you can type it after the automatic number in the **Caption** box.

3 Type a colon and a space, then copy or type the text for the picture title to follow after the figure number

4 Click away from the caption to see the figure as it will appear in the final document

Figure 1:I was struck

The captions that you create are used to create a Table of Illustrations (see page 56).

5 Repeat this procedure for each of the pictures in the document, until you have all the figures and captions

Table of Contents

When you have formatted text within the document with heading levels, you can use these to create and maintain a contents list.

1 Select **Home, Find, Go To**, then select **Page, Enter page number** "2", then click **Go To, Close**, to show that page

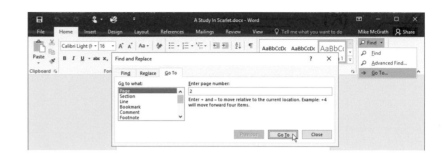

2 Select the **Insert** tab and click **Blank Page** in the Pages group, to insert a blank page for the contents list

3 Go to the new page 2, select the **References** tab, and click the **Table of Contents** button

...cont'd

4 Choose the type of table that you want, for example **Automatic Table 1** (with "Contents" as the title)

Automatic tables are generated from heading levels 1, 2 and 3. You can also build tables from custom styles, or manually selected text.

5 The Table of Contents is inserted into the document

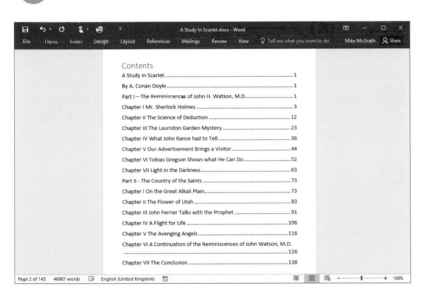

The Table of Contents must be updated to show any changes to the heading-text content, or to the page-number value.

6 When you click in the Table of Contents, its entries are grayed, to indicate they are field codes (action items)

When you hover the mouse pointer over an entry in the table, with the shift key pressed, you'll have a link to the associated section of the document.

Table of Illustrations

1 Go to the start of "Chapter I" and insert another blank page, this time for a list of illustrations

2 On the new page, type "Illustrations", select the **Home** tab, the **Styles group** button, and choose **Heading 1**

Click the **Insert** tab, then choose **Blank Page** from the Pages group to insert a blank page.

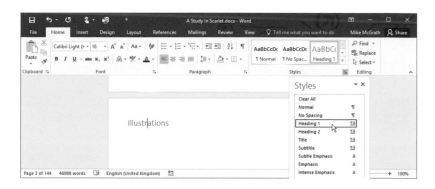

3 Press **Enter** to add a blank line, then, on the **References** tab, click the **Insert Table of Figures** button – to launch the Table of Figures dialog

4 Select the **Caption** label, i.e. "Figure", then check or clear the page number options boxes as desired

Entries for the chosen caption type, in this case "Figure", will be identified and included in the table.

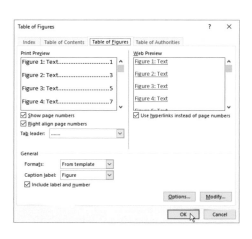

5 Click **OK** to insert the Table of Figures as shown in the Print Preview

6 The layout for the Table of Figures is similar to that of the Table of Contents created previously

There's no heading included, so any heading required must be provided separately, in this case, "Illustrations".

7 Click the table to see the grayed entries indicating that there are field codes and links to the figures

8 Right-click the table and select **Toggle Field Codes** to reveal or hide the field code for each table entry

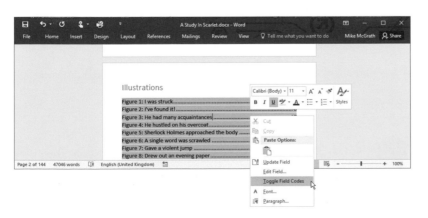

The format of the field codes for the Table of Figures indicates that it is actually a TOC (Table of Contents) based on the "Figure" label.

Insert Preface

1 Go to page 2 (the "Contents" page) and insert a blank page for the book Preface

2 On the new page, type "Preface", select the **Home** tab then the Styles group button, and choose **Heading 2**

Hot tip

If you want the Preface to appear on an odd-numbered (right-hand) page, insert a second blank page in front of it.

3 Press **Enter** and insert text from a file (see page 50). Alternatively, type the text for the Preface

4 Adjust the formatting and alignment of the text as desired, for example, selecting **Justify** for the main portion

Don't forget

Save the document whenever you make substantial changes, to avoid the risk of losing your updates.

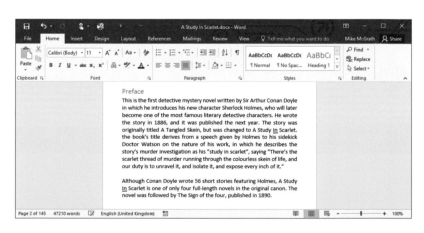

5 Select **Save** on the Quick Access Toolbar to save the latest changes that you have made

Update Table of Contents

When you make changes, such as to the Preface or the illustrations list, that include new headings (level 1, 2 or 3), the Table of Contents is affected. However, the updates will not be displayed immediately. To apply the updates:

1 Locate the Table of Contents and click anywhere within it

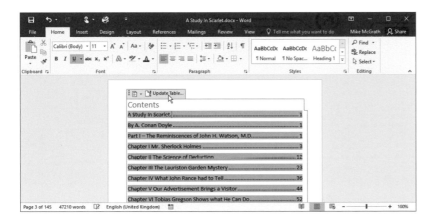

Hot tip

Whenever you add text to the document, or insert pages, the page numbers for the entries in the Table of Contents change, but the changes will not appear until you explicitly select **Update Table**.

2 Click **Update Table** at the top of the table

3 Check **Update entire table** to add new items to the table and click **OK**

4 New entries are inserted and the page numbers are updated as appropriate

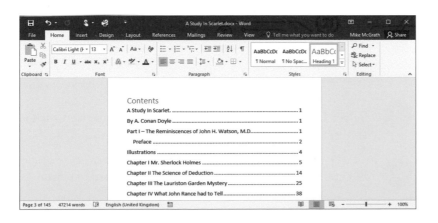

Don't forget

If you've added pages or text to your document, but have not changed the headings, select **Update page numbers only**.

Decorate the Page

You can enhance the formatting of the title page using styles or WordArt.

1 Select a section of text, expand **Styles**, and move the mouse over the options presented to preview the styles

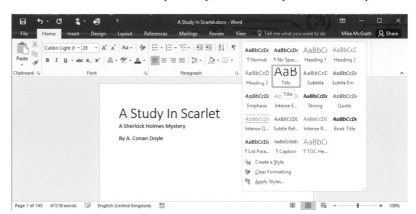

2 Click your preferred style to apply that format to the selected text. For example, select the book title and choose the **Title** style. For other selections of text you can choose styles such as **Subtitle** or one of the various other options

Title, centered

Subtitle, centered

Intense Quote

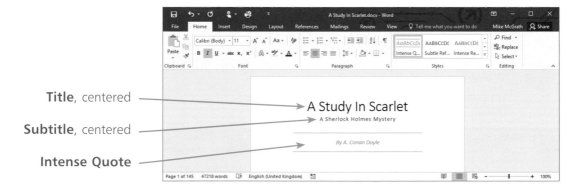

3 Select **Center** if desired. Some styles, e.g. **Intense Quote**, are centered by default

4 For more impact, select text and choose **WordArt** from the Text group on the **Insert** tab

5 Review the WordArt styles offered and select an option

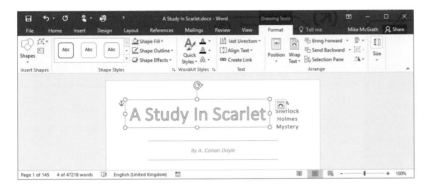

The WordArt effects are not displayed during Insert until you select a specific option. You can select a different option or clear the WordArt, if you change your mind.

6 The text is displayed in the selected style and color

7 Explore the WordArt Styles of **Text Fill**, **Text Outline** and **Text Effects**, and apply your choice

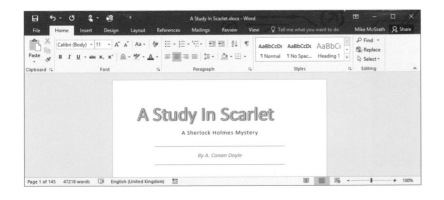

Full Reflection and **Double Wave Transform** are just two of the options offered in the **Text Effects**.

Templates

When you need a specialized form of document, you can use a predefined document template to help you get started.

1 Click the **File** tab, select **New**, and scroll through the featured templates to find one that meets your needs

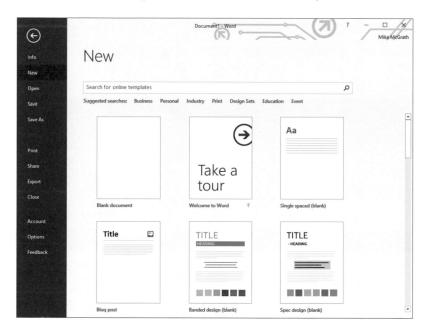

Don't forget

When you carry out a search, you will see a list of around 100 template categories, with counts of the number of templates in each category. Use this list to refine your searches.

2 If there's nothing appropriate among the samples, search for online templates, using one of the suggested searches or provide a suitable search term, e.g. "Greetings Cards"

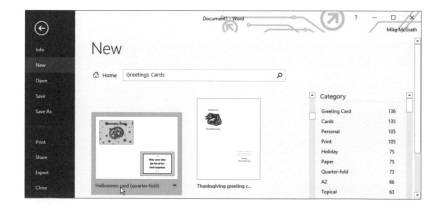

3 Click the desired template, and click the **Create** button to begin the process of downloading the template

4 When the download completes, a new document based on the downloaded template will be opened

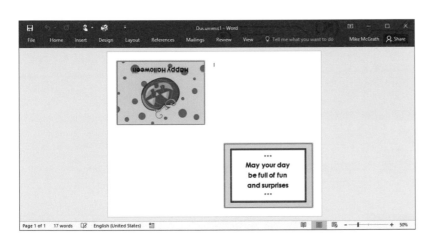

When you download a template, it is added to the list of featured templates, so it is easy to find if you need to access it in the future.

5 Modify the contents of the text box to personalize the document, and save it with an appropriate file name

This template is a four-fold document and part of the content is inverted, so that it appears correctly when folded. Other templates may be two-fold or single sheet.

Publisher

Publisher provides a higher level of desktop publishing capability, with a great variety of paper sizes and styles, including many templates for brochures, leaflets, etc., and lots of guidance.

1 Start the Publisher application, which opens with the Start screen and a selection of document templates

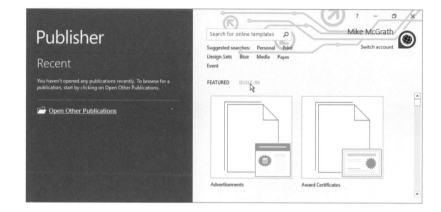

2 Explore the **Featured** and **Built-In** templates offered, or search for online templates by topic, e.g. "Birthday"

3 Review the selection provided, and select any template to see a detailed description of that design

Create a Publication

1 Choose a template, such as "Party invitation" and click the **Create** button below the detailed description

2 The template will be downloaded and a new document opens, based upon that template

3 Click the section labeled 2 & 3 to see the middle part of the card, and enter the title, description, and details, then save the document

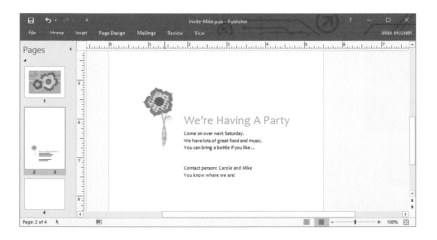

Don't forget

The greeting card is divided into four parts, each one-quarter of the physical page, making it easier to view and edit each part.

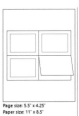
Page size: 5.5" x 4.25"
Paper size: 11" x 8.5"

65

Hot tip

Publisher offers various different sizes and layouts of greetings cards, for example:

Built-In

	1/2 A4 Top Fold	8.268 x 5.827"
	1/2 Letter Top Fold	8.5 x 5.5"
	1/4 A4 Side Fold	5.827 x 4.134"
	1/4 A4 Top Fold	5.827 x 4.134"
	1/4 Letter Side Fold	5.5 x 4.25"
	1/4 Letter Top Fold	5.5 x 4.25"
	A4 Booklet	11.693 x 8.268"

Print the Publication

1 Select pages 2, 3 and 4 to add the required text and images to those sections, then save the final document

Don't forget

Publisher shows the pages in a horizontal upright format, but will adjust the orientation of each page when you are ready to print the document.

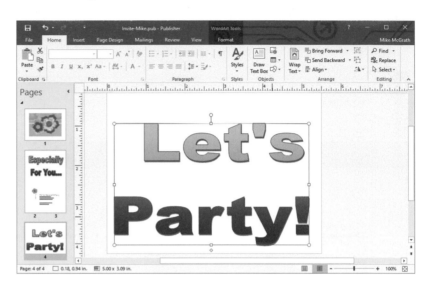

2 Select **File**, **Print**, to see the document as it appears on paper – a single sheet, with sections 2, 3 and 4 inverted

Don't forget

Once printed, the sheet is folded in half, and then folded in half again, to form the greeting card.

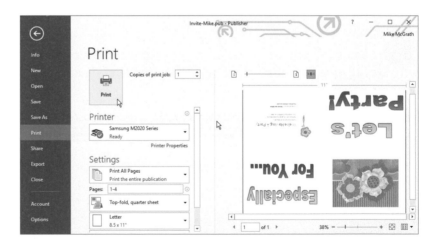

3 Adjust the settings as required, select the printer that you wish to use and then click the **Print** button

4 Calculations

This chapter looks at Excel, the spreadsheet application, and covers creating a new workbook, entering data, replicating values, formatting numbers, adding formulas and functions, and using templates.

Start Excel

To start Microsoft Excel 2016 with a fresh new spreadsheet, using the temporary name "Book1":

1 Launch the Excel 2016 application, using any of the methods described on pages 12 and 13 – via the Start menu, taskbar icon, Search box, or ask Cortana

2 By default, Excel 2016 opens at the Start screen

3 From the Excel Start screen, select **Blank workbook** to open an empty spreadsheet called "Book1"

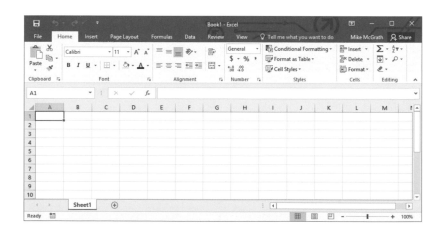

Hot tip

You can have Excel open immediately with the blank document "Book1", by-passing the Start screen. Select **File**, **Options**, **General**, then scroll down to the **Start up Options** section. Now, uncheck the box for **Show Start screen when this application starts** and click **OK**.

The spreadsheet presented is an Excel workbook that initially contains a single worksheet, which is blank. The cells that it contains are empty – all 17 million of them.

1 To move to the last row (1048576) in the worksheet, press **End**, and then press the down arrow key

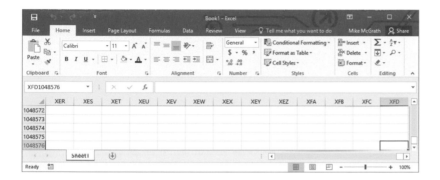

Beware

It may be impractical to utilize even a fraction of the total number of cells available, but the enlarged sheet size does give greater flexibility in designing spreadsheets. For larger amounts of data, you should use Access (see page 104).

2 To move to the last column (XFD) in the worksheet, press **End**, and then press the right arrow key

If the worksheet contains data, the action taken depends on the initial location of the selected cell.

Hot tip

There can be up to 1048576 rows and 16384 columns. This compares with 65536 rows and 256 columns in some earlier releases.

1 If the selected cell contains data, pressing **End** and then an arrow key takes you to the edge of the data area

2 If the current cell is empty, you move to the start of the adjacent data area

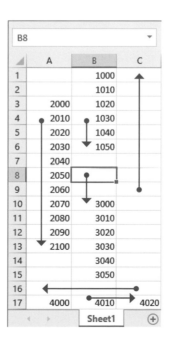

Don't forget

Movement is always in the direction of the arrow key you press after pressing the **End** key.

3 If there's no more data in that direction, you'll move to the edge of the worksheet, as with an empty worksheet

Enter Data

The most common use of spreadsheets is for financial planning; for example, to keep track of business and travel expenditure. To create a family budget:

1 Open a blank worksheet, select cell A1 and type the title for the spreadsheet, e.g. "Family Budget"

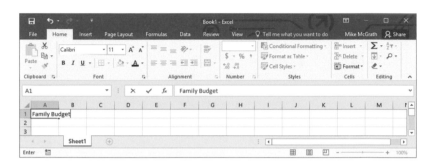

You can find ready-made budget spreadsheets and templates at the Microsoft Office website, and at other internet locations. However, it is useful to create such a spreadsheet from scratch, to illustrate the processes involved.

2 Press **Enter**, or the down key, to insert the text and move to cell A2, then type the next entry, "Income"

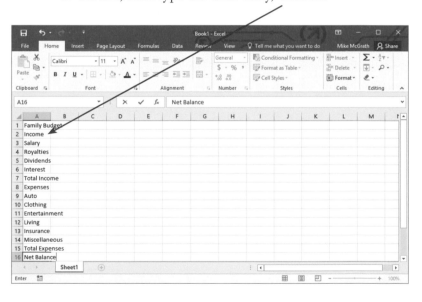

You can change the format of the labels to highlight entries such as Title, Income, and Expenses (see page 76).

3 Repeat this process to add the remaining labels for the income and expense items that you want to track, and labels for the totals and balance

If you omit an item, you can insert an additional worksheet row. For example, to include a second "Salary" income item:

1 Click a cell (e.g. C4) in the row that's just below where the new entry is required, and select **Insert**, **Insert Sheet Rows** from the Cells group on the **Home** tab

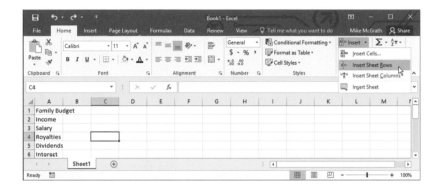

Select a vertical group of cells to insert that many rows above the selected cells. Note that you can insert one or more columns in a similar manner, by selecting **Insert**, **Insert Sheet Columns**.

2 Enter the additional label, e.g. "Salary 2nd", in A4

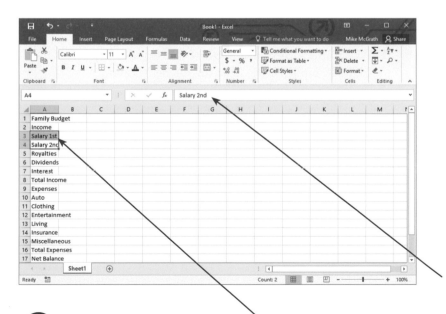

You can also select the cell and press **F2** to make changes to the content of a cell, or select the cell and modify its content on the Formula Bar.

3 Double-click an existing cell to edit or retype the entry, to change "Salary" to "Salary 1st" in A3, for example

Quick Fill

You can create one column of data, then let Excel replicate the cell contents for you. For example:

1 Enter month and values in column C, "January" in C2 and values in cells C3-C7 and C10-C15, for example

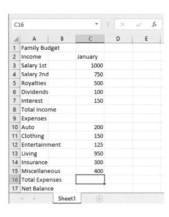
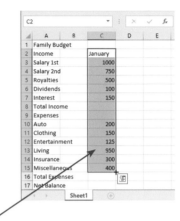

Don't forget

You can widen column A to accommodate the whole text (see the Hot Tip on page 78), then delete column B. To fully explore the data, see page 88.

2 Highlight cells C2-C15, then move the mouse pointer over the bottom right cell until the pointer changes to a **+** Fill handle

3 When the cursor becomes a **+** Fill handle, drag it to the right to replicate the cells for further months

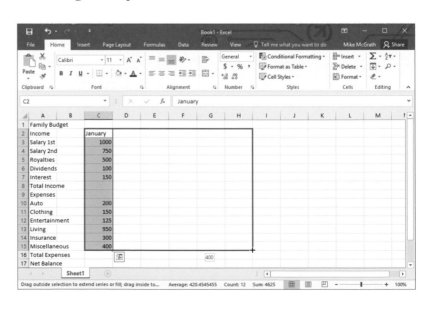

Hot tip

Click in cell C2, hold down the **Shift** key and click in cell C15 to highlight the whole column range of cells.

4 Release the **+** Fill handle when the required number of columns is indicated

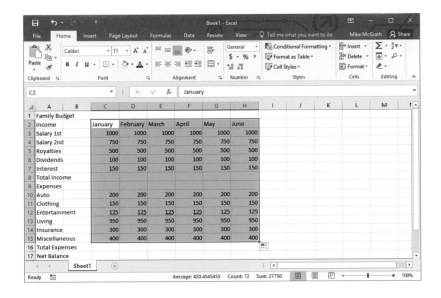

Excel detects weekdays to create a series, such as Monday, Tuesday, and it detects abbreviated names, such as Jan, Feb, or Mon, Tue, and so on.

5 Numeric values are duplicated, but the month name is detected and succeeding month names are inserted

After you release the Fill handle, an Auto Fill Options button appears. Click this to control the action, for example to replicate the formatting only, or to copy cells without devising a series such as Months.

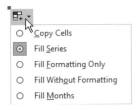

Having initialized the cells, you can edit or replace the contents of individual cells to finalize the data.

6 As you enter data into the worksheet, remember to periodically click the Save button on the Quick Access Toolbar

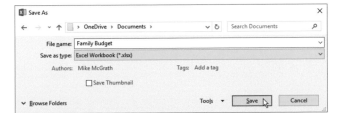

The first time you click the Save button, you'll be prompted to provide a file name in place of the default "Book1".

Sums and Differences

When you've entered the data, and made the changes required, you can introduce functions and formulas to complete the worksheet.

 1 Click cell C8 (total income for January), then select the **Home** tab, click **Editing** and then Σ **AutoSum** to sum the adjacent values

Don't forget

Numerical cells in the block immediately adjacent to the selected cell will be selected, and included in the **AutoSum** function. Always check that Excel has selected the appropriate cells.

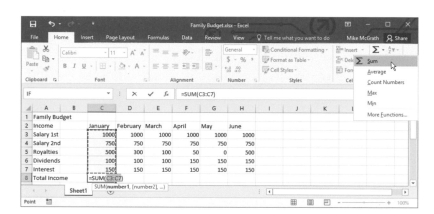

2 Press **Enter** to show the total, then repeat the procedure for cell C16 (total expenses for January)

Hot tip

The Ribbon can be collapsed and expanded in Excel 2016 just as it can in Word 2016.

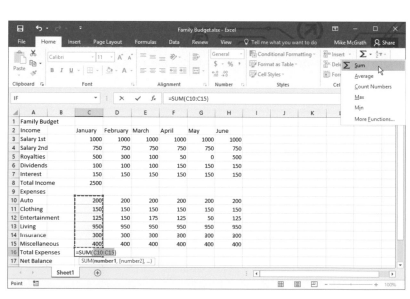

...cont'd

3 Click in cell C17 (Net Balance for January)

4 Type =, click C8, type -, then click C16 (to calculate total income minus total expenses for the month of January)

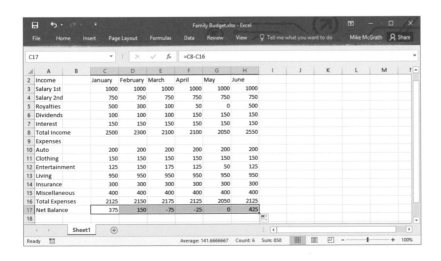

The = symbol indicates that the following text is a formula. You can type the cell references, or click on the cell itself, and Excel will enter the appropriate reference.

5 Press **Enter** to complete the formula and display the result of the sum

6 Select cell C8 and use the Fill handle to replicate the formula for the other months (February to June), and repeat this process for cells C16 and C17

When the formula is replicated, the cell references, e.g. C8:C16, are incremented to D8:D16, E8:E16, etc.

Formatting

1 Click A1 (the title cell), then select the **Home** tab, choose a larger font size, and select a font effect, such as Bold

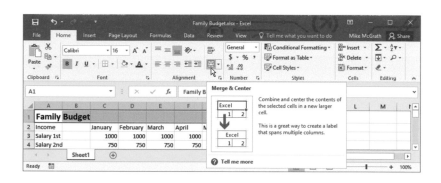

Hot tip

Changing the format for various parts of the worksheet can make it easier to review and assess the results.

Don't forget

You can change each cell individually, or press **Ctrl** and click each of the cells to select them, then apply the changes to all the cells at once.

2 Press **Shift**, and click H1 to highlight the row across the data, then click the **Merge & Center** button

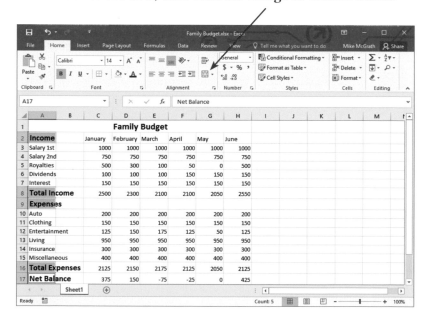

3 Click the Categories and Totals labels (e.g. A2, A8, A9, A16, A17), and change the font size and effects

4 Or click **Cell Styles** to pick a suitable style

...cont'd

To emphasize the "Net Balance" values for each month:

1 Select the range of cells, e.g. C17:H17

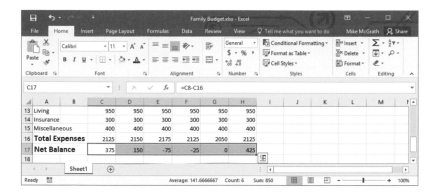

2 Select **Styles, Conditional Formatting, Color Scales** and choose one of the swatches. For example, you might select the Green–Yellow–Red color scale

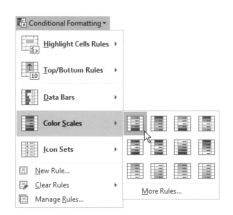

3 The cells are colored and shaded appropriately for the values that they contain

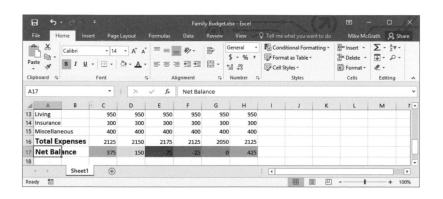

Rounding Up

You can use Excel functions, such as Round Up or Ceiling, to adjust the solutions of numerical problems, such as the number of tiles needed to cover the floor area of a room.

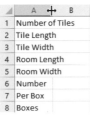

Hot tip

Double-click the separator bar between the A and B headings to extend the column width to fit the longest entry.

1 Open a new, blank worksheet, and enter these labels in the first column:

Number of Tiles
Tile Length
Tile Width
Room Length
Room Width
Number
Per Box
Boxes

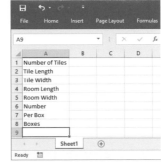

2 Enter sample sizes in cells B2:B5, making sure that you use the same units for the tile and room dimensions

3 In cell B6, type the formula **=(B4/B2)*(B5/B3)**

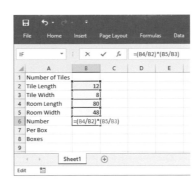

Don't forget

The number of tiles in cell B6 is the calculated quantity of tiles required to cover the floor space exactly.

4 In cell B8, type the formula **=B6/B7**

Beware

You need to calculate whole numbers of tiles, allowing for wastage where tiles need to be cut to fit.

For these figures, and on the basis of these calculations, you might think 5 boxes would be sufficient. However, if you fit the tiles to the area, you find that some tiles have to be trimmed. The wastage leaves part of the area uncovered.

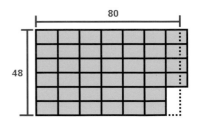

To ensure that there are enough whole tiles to completely cover the area, you need to round up the evaluations:

1 Copy B2:B8 to C2:C8, and, in cell C6, type the formula **=CEILING(C4/C2,1)*CEILING(C5/C3,1)**

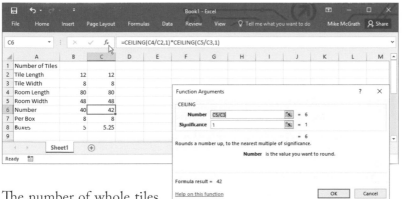

The number of whole tiles increases to 42, which will now cover the complete floor area, even after cutting.

This gives 5.25 boxes. Assuming that boxes must be purchased in whole numbers, this result also needs rounding up.

Click the *fx* button to open the Function Arguments dialog.

2 Copy C2:C8 to D2:D8, and in cell D8, type the formula **=ROUNDUP(D6/D7,0)** to get the result of 6 boxes

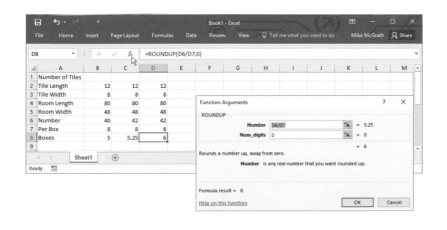

The ROUNDUP function is another way to adjust values. Here, it is used to round up the result to zero decimal places, which also gives the next highest integer.

Find a Function

There are a large number of functions available in Excel. They are organized into a library of categories to make it easier to find the particular function you need.

1 Select the **Formulas** tab to show the Function Library

Hot tip

You can click the **More Functions** button to display a secondary list of categories.

2 Click a category in the Function Library for an alphabetic list of functions it offers. For example, click the **Logical** category

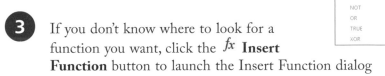

3 If you don't know where to look for a function you want, click the *fx* **Insert Function** button to launch the Insert Function dialog

4 In the Insert Function dialog, you can type a description of a function you are seeking in the **Search for a function** box. For example, type "Loan Repayment" then press **Go** and choose from the list of recommended functions

Hot tip

Enter keywords related to the activity you want to perform, and Excel will list all potentially relevant functions.

5 Alternatively, you can click the arrow button by the **Or select a category** box and choose from the drop-down list of categories, then pick a function from the list offered. For example, choose the "Financial" category

6 Choose a function, such as the **PMT** function, then click the **OK** button to launch the Function Arguments dialog

The function arguments for the selected function are shown, and a brief description is provided.

7 Type the values for the arguments **Rate** (interest rate per period of loan), **Nper** (number of repayments), and **PV** (present value of loan amount), then press **OK**

You can optionally provide a final value, **Fv** (the cash balance), and also specify the **Type** (payments made at the start or the end of each period).

8 The function is inserted into the worksheet, and the result is displayed as a negative figure (indicating a payment)

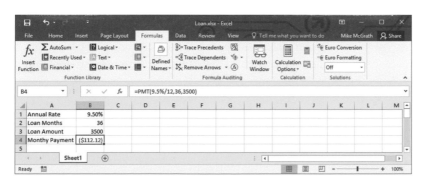

Goal Seeking

Using the **PMT** function, you can establish the monthly payments required to pay off a long-term loan over 25 years, for example.

To calculate payments for an interest-only loan, set **Fv** (see page 81) to the same value as the loan amount.

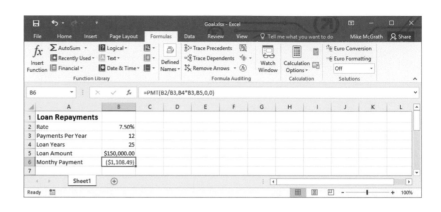

Suppose, however, you'd like to know how many years it will take to pay off the loan if you increase the payments to $1500?

 One way to establish this is by trial and error, adjusting the number of years until you get the required payment

You would carry on refining your estimate, e.g. trying 12 then 14, to discover that the correct answer lies between these two periods.

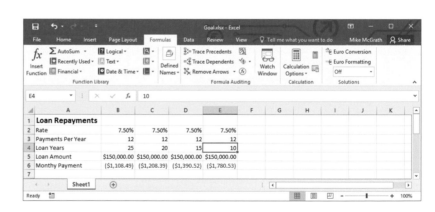

Try 20 years, then 15 years, then 10 years, the payment then goes above $1500. So the appropriate period would be between 10 and 15 years

However, Excel provides an automatic way to apply this type of process, and this can give you an exact answer very quickly.

1 Click the cell containing the function, then select the **Data** tab, and click the **What-If Analysis** button in the Forecast group

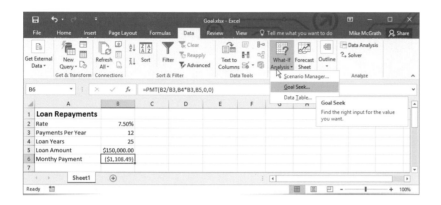

Use the **Scenario Manager** to create a set of results for a range of values, such as 10, 15 and 20 years of repayments.

2 Select the **Goal Seek** option and specify the required result as -1500 (the payment per month) and the change to cell B4 (the number of years for full repayment)

You must specify the target payment as a negative value, since it is a repayment, otherwise **Goal Seek** will be unable to find a solution:

3 **Goal Seek** tries out various values for the changing cell, until the desired solution is found

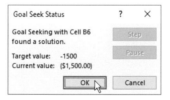

4 Click **OK** to see the solution appear in the worksheet

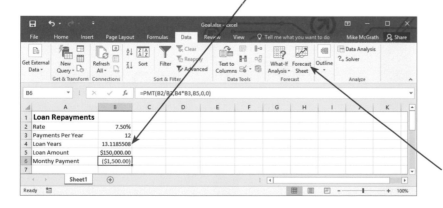

You can select a range of data, then click **Forecast Sheet** to generate a quick pop-up forecast.

Templates

1 Select the **File** tab and click the **New** button

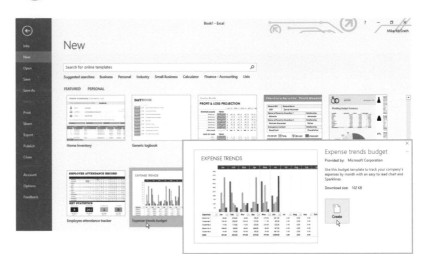

You can get started with your worksheet by using one of the ready-made templates, which are offered for many common requirements.

2 Select any of the **Featured** templates to view its content, and click **Create** to open a document using the template

3 Alternatively, select a category to review the templates from Microsoft Office Online

4 Choose a template to see the layout, then click **Create** to download your preferred template and open a document using that template

Check periodically to find out what new templates have been added to the Office Online website (**www.office.com**).

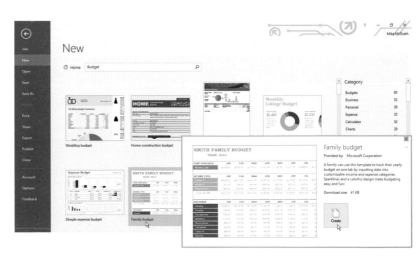

5 Manage Data

Excel also manages data, so we will look at importing data, applying sorts and filters, and selecting specific sets of data. The data can be used to create a chart, or you can arrange the data in tables, insert totals and computations, and look up values. Some editions of Office include Access, which offers full database management functions.

Import Data

You don't always need to type in all the information in your worksheets if the data is already available in another application. For example, to import data from a delimited text file:

1 Click the **File** tab and select **Open**

Identify the appropriate file type to select from, in this case, "Text Files".

2 Select the file that contains the data you wish to import and click **Open** to start the Text Import Wizard, which recognizes the delimited file. Click **Next** to continue

Select **My data has headers** if appropriate, so that the header line is treated separately.

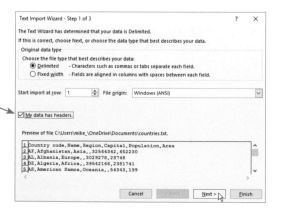

...cont'd

3 Check the delimiter type (e.g. **Comma**) and click **Next**

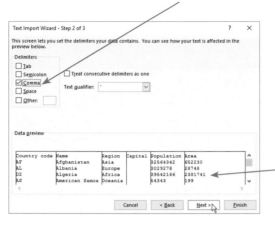

Hot tip

When you choose a delimiter, you can see the effect on the text in the preview area.

4 Adjust column formats, if required, then click **Finish**

Don't forget

The default format is **General**, which will handle most situations, but you can select specific data formats where appropriate.

5 The data is presented in the form of an Excel worksheet

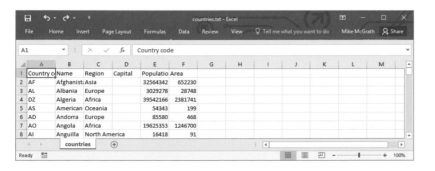

Hot tip

Excel can retrieve data from any application that can create files in a delimited text file format, such as CSV (comma-separated values), or from database systems, such as SQL Server, Access, dBase, FoxPro, Oracle, and Paradox.

Explore the Data

Select the **File** tab, click **Save As** and choose file type Excel Workbook, to save the data as a standard Excel file.

1 Double-click or drag the separators between the columns to reveal more of the data they contain

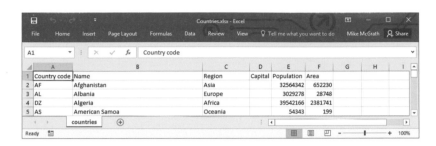

2 Select the **View** tab, click **Freeze Panes** in the Window group, and select **Freeze Top Row**

Freezing the top row makes the headings it contains visible, whichever part of the worksheet is being displayed.

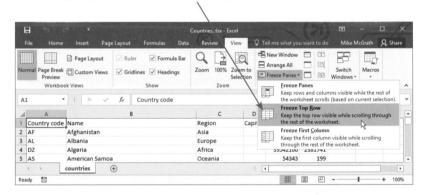

3 Press **Ctrl + End** to move to the last cell in the data area and again, adjusting column widths as desired

This will show you how many rows and columns there are in the data (in this example, 249 rows and 6 columns).

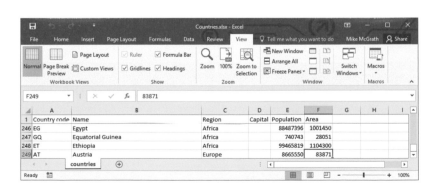

Sort

1 Click a cell in the "Country code" column, select the **Data** tab and click **A-Z** to sort alphabetically, ascending

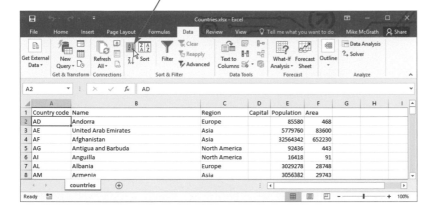

You can also select the **Sort** options from within the Editing group on the **Home** tab.

2 Click a cell in the "Population" column and click the **Z-A** button to sort numerically, descending (highest to lowest)

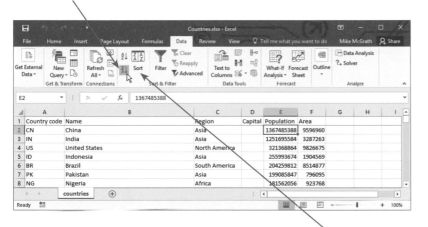

If you click in a single cell, Excel will select all the surrounding data and sort the rows of contiguous data into the required order.

3 To sort by more than one value, first click the **Sort** button to launch the Sort dialog box

You can sort the data into sequence using several levels of values.

...cont'd

4 Click the arrow in the **Sort by** box and select the main sort value, for example "Region"

If a selection of the worksheet is highlighted when you click one of the buttons, the sort may be restricted to the selected data.

5 Click the **Add Level** button and select the additional sort values, for example "Population"

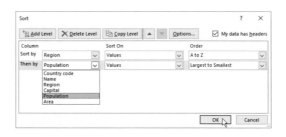

6 Change the sort sequence, if needed, then click **OK** to sort the data here by "Region" and by "Population"

For data organized by columns, rather than rows, click the **Options** button and select **Sort left to right**.

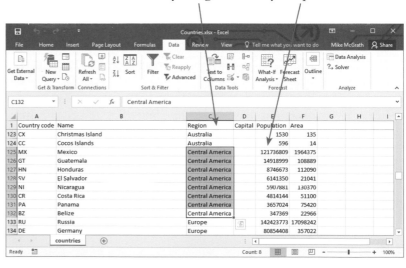

Filters

You can filter the data to hide entries that are not of immediate interest.

1 Click a cell within the data area, select the **Data** tab and click the **Filter** button in the Sort & Filter group

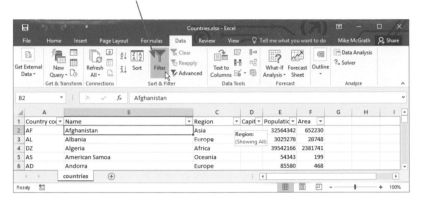

You can also select the **Filter** button from within the Editing group on the **Home** tab (see page 89).

2 Click a filter icon, e.g. "Region", to display its **AutoFilter**

3 Uncheck the **Select All** box, to deselect all entries, then select the specific entry you want, e.g. check "Oceania"

4 Click **OK** to apply the filter

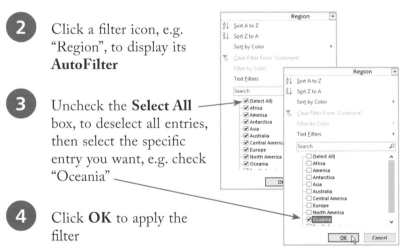

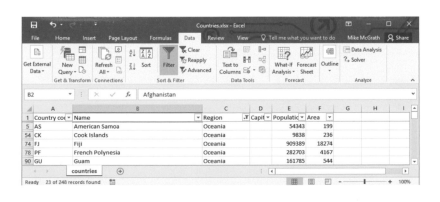

Filtering is turned on, and a filter icon (an arrow) is added to each heading, with an initial setting of **Showing All**.

Number Filters

Don't forget

You can set number filters to specify a level at which to accept or reject entries, or choose an option, such as accepting the top ten entries.

1 Display the **AutoFilter** for "Population", and choose all entries **Greater Than Or Equal To...** a value of 100,000

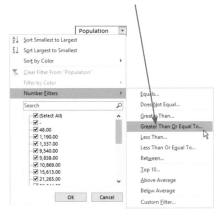

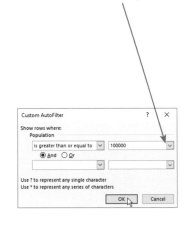

2 The filter button icon is changed, to show that filtering is in effect for the modified **AutoFilter** column

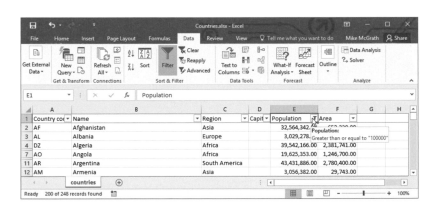

Hot tip

Use **Format Cells** on the **Home** tab to include a comma separator in columns containing numeric data.

Beware

If you click the **Filter** button on the **Data** tab, or the **Home** tab, it will remove all the filters and delete all filter settings.

3 Click a filter icon and select the **Clear Filter** option to remove the filter for a particular column

4 The filter icon for that column reverts to an arrow, and the **Showing All** option will be applied

Select Specific Data

Suppose you want to select only countries with a large population, you can hide away information that's not relevant for that purpose:

1 Use the **AutoFilter** on the "Population" column to display only countries whose population **Is Greater Than** a value of 150 million

2 Select all irrelevant columns. For example, hold down **Ctrl** and click columns: A ("Country codes"), C ("Region"), D ("Capital"), and F ("Area")

3 Now, select the **Home** tab and click **Format**, **Hide & Unhide**, **Hide Columns** – to display only relevant data

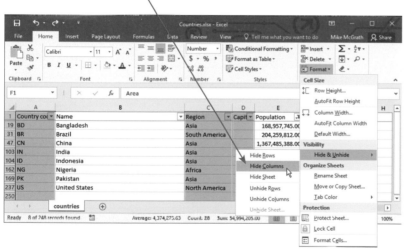

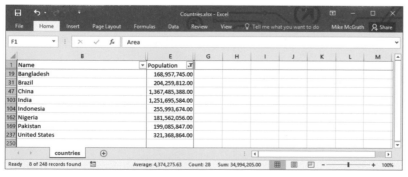

Hot tip

Filter the rows and hide selected columns to remove the data not needed at the moment from view.

Don't forget

This places the column of country "Name" adjacent to the column of "Population", ready for further analysis – creating a chart, for example. To help with this, you might sort the information, e.g. in descending numeric order of "Population".

Create a Chart

1 Highlight the data (including headers), then select the **Insert** tab and click the Charts group arrow button

Hot tip

Explore each category of chart type to discover numerous sub-type options.

Office 2016 offers six new chart types to choose from.

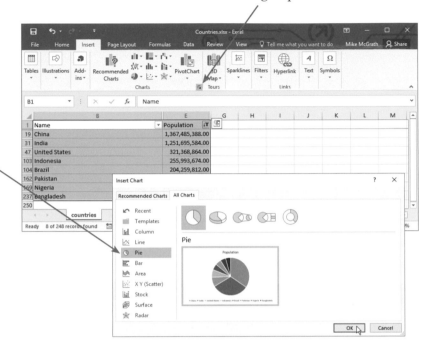

2 Choose the chart type you require, in this case a **Pie** chart

Hot tip

When you've created a chart, the **Chart Tools Design** and **Format** tabs are displayed, where you can select other Chart Styles or use the **Change Chart Type** button to try one of the other chart options.

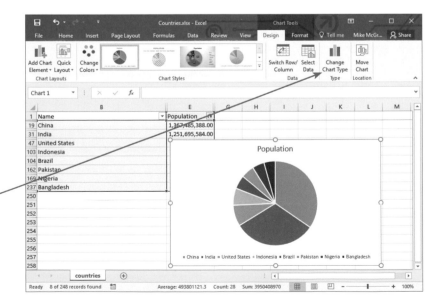

...cont'd

3 Choose a Chart Style, then right-click on the population data columns and select **Format Data Labels...**

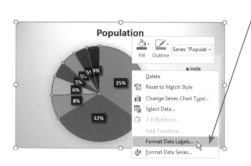

You can also use the **Chart Tools**, **Format** tab to customize the appearance of a chart.

4 Adjust the column labels to your preference. For example, add **Legend key** and choose **Best Fit**

5 Click on any component, then click it again to edit its content. For example, edit the "Population" title component's text content

6 Click on any component, then move the cursor to its bounding box to grab the component and reposition it in the chart. For example, drag the chart title to the right

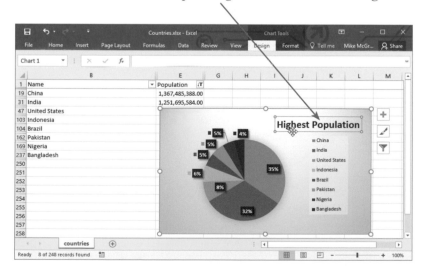

You can select the **Move Chart** button on the **Chart Tools**, **Design** tab to place the chart on a separate worksheet.

Import a List

The "Countries" worksheet includes an empty "Capital" column. This data is listed in a text file, of "Country codes" and their "Capital" cities, which can be imported into the worksheet.

1 Select a cell marking the start of an empty section of the worksheet, and then click the **Data** tab

Don't forget

In the sample worksheet, the original "Capital" column has no data.

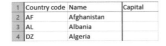

1	Country code	Name	Capital
2	AF	Afghanistan	
3	AL	Albania	
4	DZ	Algeria	

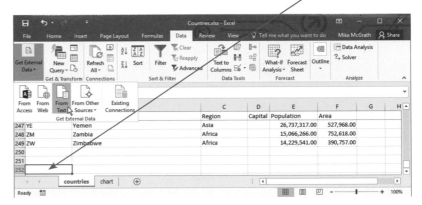

2 Click **Get External Data** and choose **From Text**

3 Locate the text file, click **Import**, then employ the Text Import Wizard (see pages 86-87)

4 Click **OK** to place the data in the current worksheet, at the location you initially selected

Don't forget

The text list is imported into the worksheet as a named range, using the name of the external text file, e.g. "capitals".

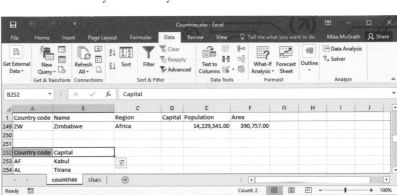

Create a Table

1 Click a cell within the data range, select the **Insert** tab, then click the **Tables, Table** button

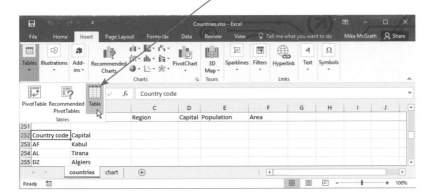

Don't forget

When you create a table from a data range, any connection with the external data source will be removed.

2 Click **OK** to confirm the range and accept the headers

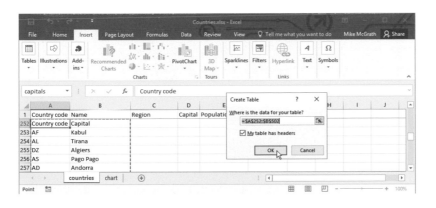

Hot tip

To make it easier to manage and analyze the data in the list, you can turn the range of cells into an Excel table.

3 The table will be created using the default style

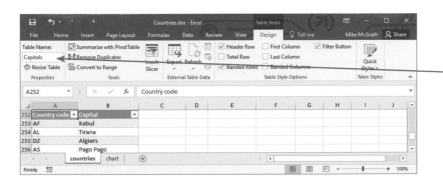

Hot tip

Change the default name ("Table1" or similar) to something that's more relevant to the content, in this case "Capitals".

Add Totals to Table

Hot tip

Convert the range of country data into table form, then add totals.

1 Click a cell within the original country data and select **Insert**, **Table**, then rename the new table as "Countries"

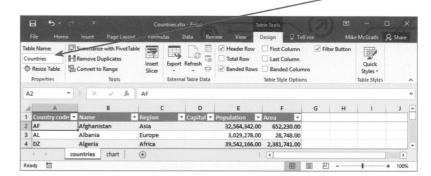

2 Select the **Table Tools**, **Design** tab, then check the box for the **Total Row**, to add that row at the end of the table

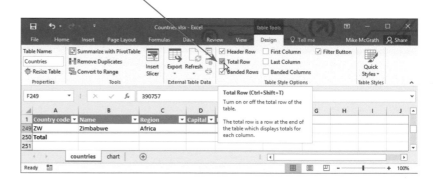

Don't forget

The functions that you choose are entered into the formula as numbered sub-functions of the **Subtotal** function:
101 (Average)
102 (Count numbers)
103 (Count)
104 (Max)
105 (Min)
107 (StdDev)
109 (Sum)
110 (Variance)

3 Select the "Name" column cell on the **Total Row**, click its arrow button and choose a function, e.g. choose **Count**

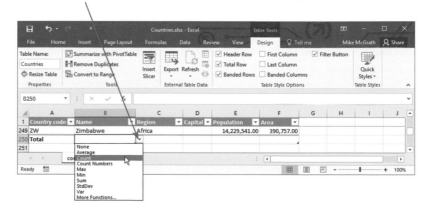

4 See the total count of country names appear, then select the **Sum** function for a column with numerical values, such as the "Population" column to see total population

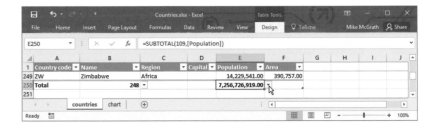

5 You can use functions, such as **Max** (sub-function 104) and **Min** (sub-function 105) to show the range of values in a column, e.g. to display the largest country "Area"

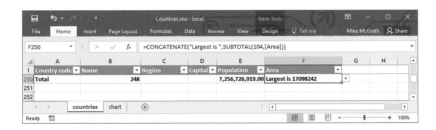

6 When a column contains a set of discrete values, such as "Region", you can calculate the number of unique values it contains, e.g. to display the unique number of "Region"

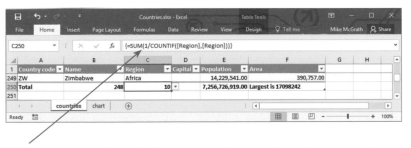

This is an array formula that counts the number of times each particular value in the column is repeated, and uses these repeats to build up a count of the number of distinct values.

Hot tip

Do not use the column and row labels to specify cells and ranges. Instead, use the table header name for the column (enclosed in square brackets).

Don't forget

You can use any Excel function in the total boxes, not just sub-functions of the **Subtotal** function.

Hot tip

Type an array formula without the enclosing { } curly braces, then press **Ctrl + Shift + Enter** (instead of the usual **Enter**) and the braces are added automatically.

Computed Column

You can add a column to the table without affecting other ranges, data, or tables in the worksheet.

1 Click in the "Area" column, select the **Home** tab, click **Insert**, and choose **Insert Table Columns to the Right**

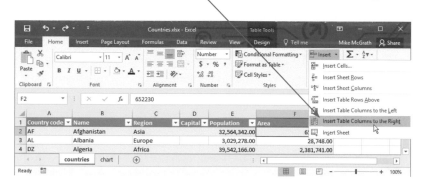

Hot tip

If you select a cell in the last column of the table, you can insert a column to the left or the right, otherwise you can only insert a column to the left of the selected cell.

2 The new column is inserted, initially named "Column1"

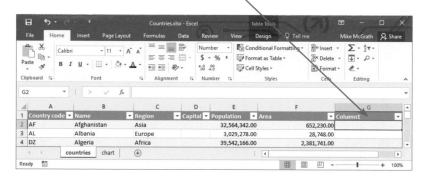

Don't forget

The column names are used in the formulas, so it is best to choose meaningful names.

3 Select the new column header, type a new name, such as "Density", and press **Enter**

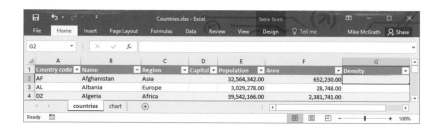

4 Click in the first cell of the "Density" column and type =, then click the "Population" column cell in the same row

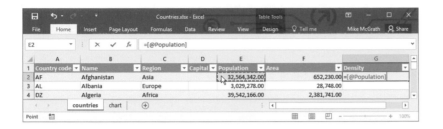

The cell that you select is referenced as the current row of the "Population" column, in the formula as: **[@Population]**.

5 Type /, then click the "Area" column cell in the same row

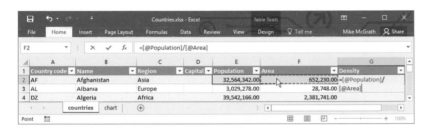

The next cell you select is referenced as: **[@Area]**.

6 Press **Enter**. The expression is evaluated and copied to all the other cells in the table's "Density" column

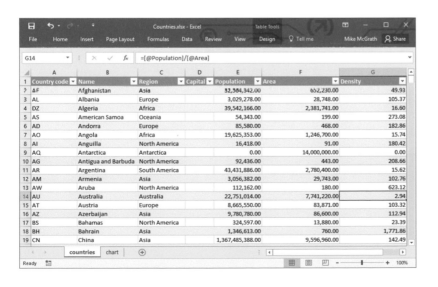

The result is the population density, the number of people per square kilometer, formatted to two decimal places.

Table Lookup

The example "Countries" table contains a column for the name of the capital city of each country, which is presently empty:

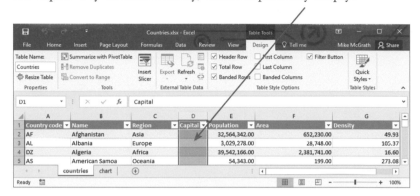

The capital city names are stored in the separate "Capitals" table, which is a list that was imported into the worksheet earlier:

The "Capitals" table was created on pages 96-97.

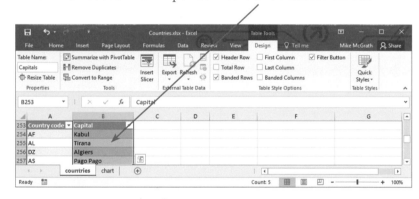

An Excel function named **VLOOKUP** (vertical lookup) can be used to populate the empty "Capital" column in the "Countries" table:

 Click the first cell of the "Capital" column in the "Countries" table and type the expression **=VLOOKUP(**

VLOOKUP is the vertical-lookup function, used to seek values stored in a table column. There is also a **HLOOKUP** horizontal-lookup function you can use to seek values stored in a table row.

2 Click the first cell in the "Country code" column of the "Countries" table, to specify that you want the function to search for country code values – a reference to the "Country code" column gets added to the formula

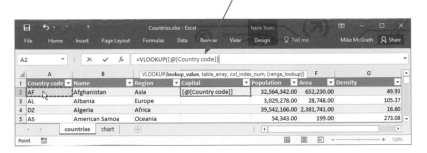

Hot tip

It doesn't matter whether the country codes are listed in the same order within each table, as the **VLOOKUP** function looks through the entire first column of the specified target table ("Capitals" in this case) to find a match for each country code in turn.

3 Complete the formula by specifying the table in which to search (**Capitals**), the column number in that table whose value is sought (**2**), and to only accept an exact match (**0**)

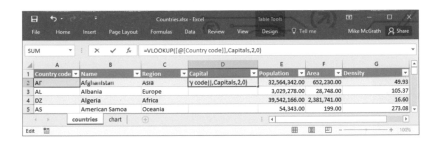

Beware

You must insert a comma in the formula between each value specified to the **VLOOKUP** function.

4 Press **Enter** to fill the empty column with the correct capital names that are associated with each country code

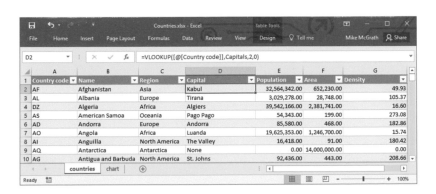

Manage Data using Access

If you have large amounts of data, or complex functions to handle, you may require the more comprehensive facilities in Access 2016.

1 Select **Access** from the Start menu or the taskbar, and you'll be greeted by a range of database template tiles

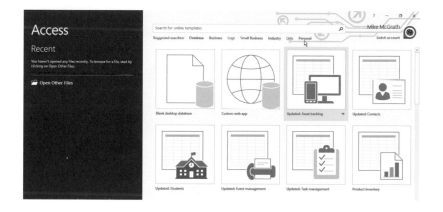

2 Select a category, such as **Personal**, to display a list of related templates available on the internet

Hot tip

You'll find Access 2016 in Office Professional 2016, and Office 365. It appears only on the Start menu, but you can also pin it to the taskbar beside your other Office app launcher icons.

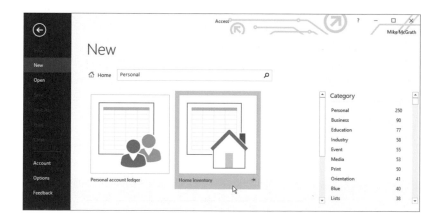

3 Select any template tile to view a description of what that template can be used for

4 When you've found the template that you want to use, specify a file name and preferred location on your system, or accept the suggested defaults

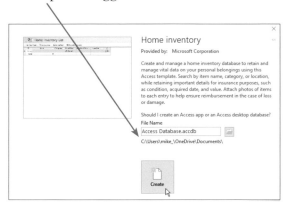

The template will be stored in the recent templates area and will be immediately available for reuse when you select **File**, **New** to create a database.

5 Click the **Create** button to download that template to your computer

6 Access prepares the template for use as a new database, but the database is opened with active content disabled

7 Click **Enable Content** to enable the VBA macros in the template and make the database ready for updating

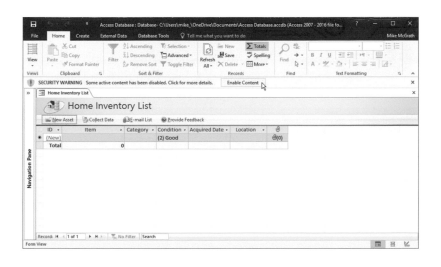

Do not enable content in databases that you download from internet websites, unless you are sure that the source of the file is trustworthy.

Add Records

1 Click the **New Asset** button to launch the Asset Details dialog, in which you can add a record to the database

You can type directly into the cells of the asset table if you prefer, rather than using the form.

2 Enter the details for the item, selecting from a list of values on fields with a drop-down arrow button, e.g. **Category**

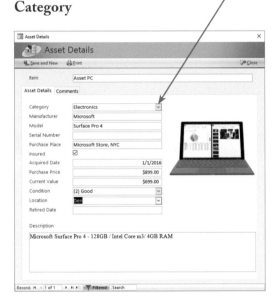

You can attach links to associated documents, or photos of the asset if you wish, as seen here.

3 Click **Save and New**, to save the current record and then begin a new record, or click **Close** to return to the list

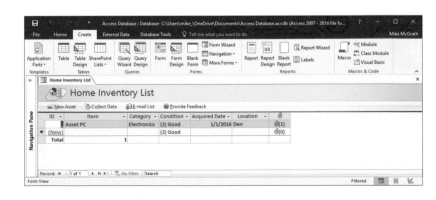

The current record is automatically saved when you click **Close**, even if all the details are not completed.

6 Presentations

Build a presentation, slide by slide, apply themes to create a consistent effect, and use animation to focus attention on particular points. Use a second monitor for a presenter view, and take advantage of templates, built-in or downloaded, and print handouts for the presentation. Rehearse the show to get timings, and create an automatic show.

Start a Presentation

To start PowerPoint 2016 and create a presentation:

1 Launch the PowerPoint application, using any of the methods described on pages 12 and 13 – via the Start menu, taskbar icon, Search box, or ask Cortana

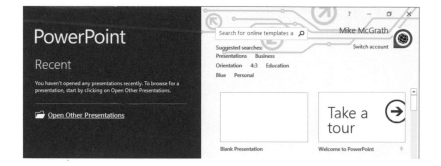

Hot tip

When PowerPoint opens, it presents a single, blank title slide, ready for you to begin a new presentation.

2 Click **Blank Presentation** to open a new presentation at the first slide – to add titles

3 Now, select **Click to add title**, then type the title for your slide show, e.g. "Origami"

4 Next, select **Click to add subtitle**, and type the subtitle for your slide show, e.g. "The Japanese Art of Paper Folding"

Don't forget

By default, the presentation starts with a title slide, where two text boxes are predefined. If you don't want a particular text box, just ignore it – it won't appear on the slide unless you edit the text.

...cont'd

5 Select the **Home** tab and click the **New Slide** button in the Slides group

6 Choose **Title and Content** to add a new slide that provides text boxes for a title and content

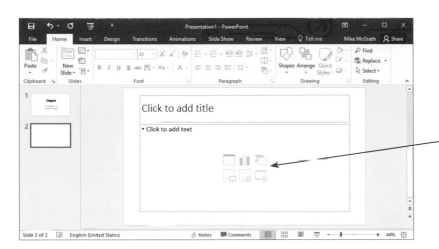

Hot tip

The new **Title and Content** slide has option buttons to **Insert Table**, **Insert Chart**, **Insert a SmartArt Graphic**, **Pictures**, **Online Pictures**, or **Insert Video**. See page 111 for an example.

7 Click on the prompts and add the title "The History of Origami", then type bullet points to give the details

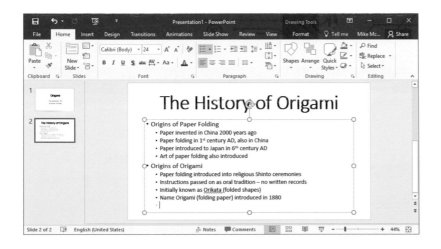

Don't forget

Click within a bullet item and press **Shift + Tab** to promote it (move up) to the next higher level.

Press **Alt + Shift + Left Arrow** to demote.

8 Press **Enter** to add a new bullet item, and then press the **Tab** key to move to the next lower level of bullet items

Expand the Slide

1 Click the 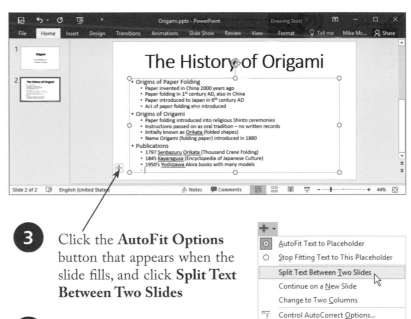 button to **Save** your presentation

2 Continue to add items and you'll see the text size and spacing adjusts to fit the text onto the slide

Alternatively, you can choose options to **Stop Fitting Text to This Placeholder**, to **Continue on a New Slide**, or **Change to Two Columns** layout.

3 Click the **AutoFit Options** button that appears when the slide fills, and click **Split Text Between Two Slides**

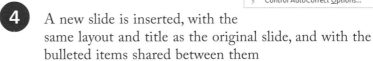

4 A new slide is inserted, with the same layout and title as the original slide, and with the bulleted items shared between them

The text size and spacing will be readjusted to take advantage of the extra space available.

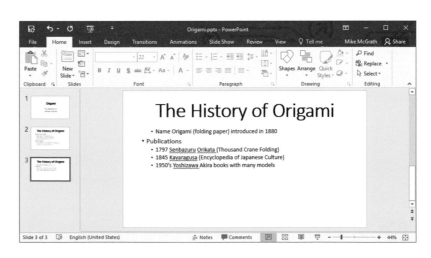

Insert a Picture

1 Select the **Home** tab, then click the arrow on the **New Slide** button in the Slides group to display the options

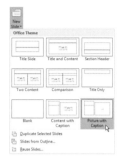

2 Choose a slide layout, such as **Picture with Caption**

3 Now select **Click icon to add picture**

Hot tip

There are nine standard layouts for slides, so you can select the one that's most appropriate for the specific content planned for each slide.

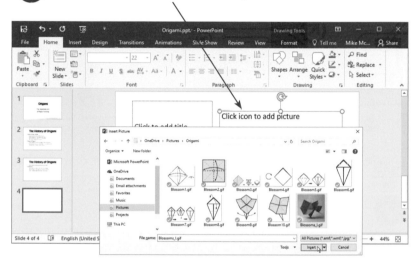

Don't forget

The title and the text you add provide the caption for the inserted image.

111

4 Locate and select the image file and click **Insert**, then select in turn **Click to add title**, and **Click to add text**

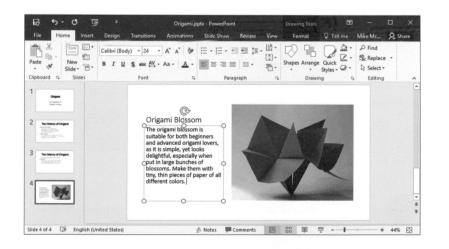

Don't forget

Insert the other slides needed to complete your presentation.

Apply a Theme

The default slides have a plain background, but you can choose a more attractive theme and apply it to all the slides you've created.

 Select the **Design** tab, then move the mouse pointer over each of the themes to see the effect

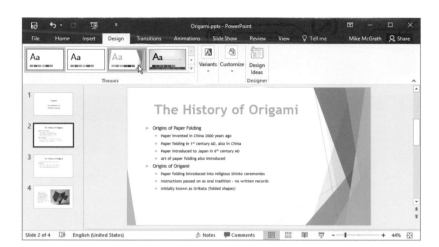

2 You can scroll the list to display additional themes, change the colors, fonts, and effects for the current theme, and modify the type of background style it uses

3 When you find a theme you like, click your preferred theme to apply it to all slides in the presentation

To select the transition effects between slides:

1 Select the
Transitions
tab, then
click the
**Transition
to This Slide**
down arrow
to view all
possible
effects

When you select a
transition, the **Effects
Options** button
becomes enabled,
so you can choose
variations of that
transition.

2 Select any effect then click the **Preview** button to see
how it looks and assign it to the current slide

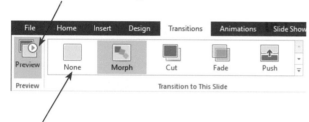

3 Click **None** after running a preview if you don't want to
assign the effect to the slide

By default, each slide advances to the next slide when you press
the mouse key, but you can adjust the setting for individual slides.

1 Uncheck the **Advance Slide**, **On Mouse Click** box to
disable the mouse-key for the current slide

2 Check the **After** box and
specify a delay time

3 Click the **Apply To All** button to apply the settings to all
the slides in the presentation

If you have specified
animation effects for
individual elements on
a slide (see page 114),
the Advance function
invokes the next
animation, rather than
the next slide.

Whatever the setting, you can always advance the slide show by
pressing one of the keyboard shortcuts, such as **N** (next), **Enter**,
Page Down, **Right Arrow**, or **Spacebar**.

Animations

You can apply animation effects to individual parts of a slide.

1 Select the **Animations** tab, pick a slide with bullet items, and note that the tab items are grayed out (inactive)

2 Select any object within the current slide you wish to animate, to see the **Animations** tab items become active

There is a choice of **Entrance**, **Emphasis**, or **Exit** animations, and the **Effect Options** button lets you choose how they should be applied.

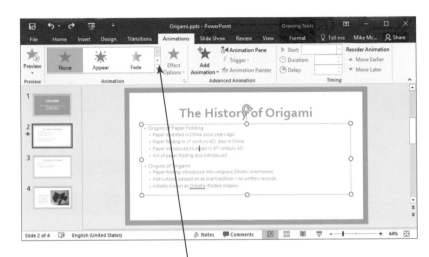

3 Click the down-arrow on the Animation group selection box, then choose an animation to see how it looks and assign it to the current slide. For example, choose **Fly In**

Select **Add Animation** in the Advanced Animation group, if you want to apply additional effects to the slide.

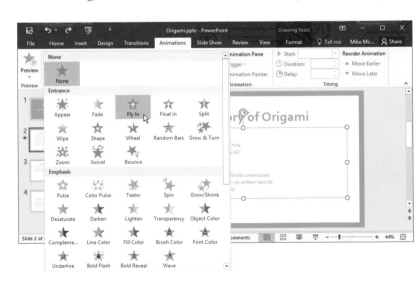

Run the Show

When you've added all the slides you need, you can try running
the complete show, to see the overall effect.

1 Select the **Slide Show** tab and click the **From Beginning**
button in the Start Slide Show group

You can also press **F5** to
run the slide show from
the beginning, press
Shift + F5 to run from
the current slide, or press
Esc to terminate.

2 The slides are displayed full-screen, with the transition
and animation effects that you selected

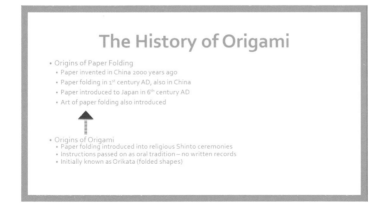

You'll see your selected
transition effects and
selected animations. In
this case, **Fly In** text from
the bottom of the slide.

When the slide show
finishes, a black screen
is presented, with the
message: **End of slide
show, click to exit**.

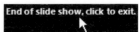

3 Click the mouse or keyboard shortcut to advance the slide
show, animation by animation, or wait the specified time

4 Review each slide in turn through to the end of the show

Other Views

1 Select the **View** tab and select **Slide Sorter** to display all the slides, so that you can rearrange their sequence

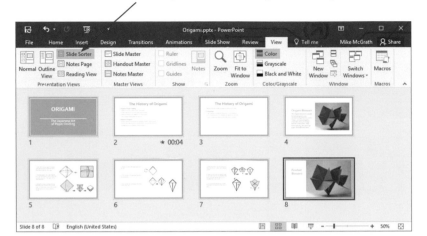

This view is helpful when you have a large number of slides, since you can simply drag slides into their new positions.

There's also a **Reading View** button, provided in the Presentation Views group on the **View** tab, which allows you to view the slide show in an easily readable format.

2 Select the **Notes Page** view to see the current slide with its notes (information and prompts for the presenter)

In Notes Page view, each slide and its notes will be displayed on a single sheet, which can be printed to make a very useful handout.

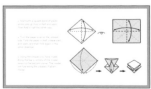

Every crease needs to be flattened quite well for a successful model. You can reinforce a crease by running the side of your thumbnail along the fold, or using a tool such as the end of a plastic ruler, that won't damage the paper.

3 Click the 🔍 **Zoom** button, or drag the slider on the zoom bar, to examine the slide or notes in detail

4 Click the ⊡ **Fit to Window** button, or select **Fit** and click **OK** on the Zoom menu, to resize the view and make the whole page visible

5 To switch back to the view with slide bar and current slide, click the **Normal** button

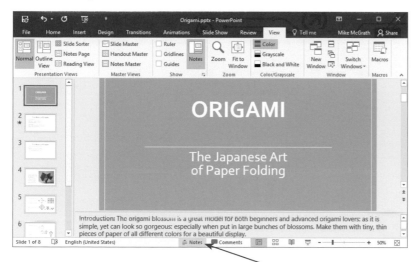

Beware

The view you select will be retained when you select another tab, so you should revert to the required view before leaving.

6 To reveal more of the notes area, click the **Notes** button on the status bar, then drag the separator bar upwards

7 Click the **Outline View** button to see the text content of the slides given in a summary view of the presentation

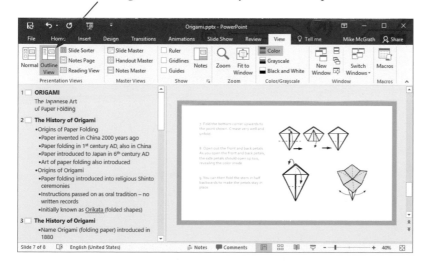

Hot tip

The buttons to the left of the Zoom bar are another way to select **Normal**, **Slide Sorter**, **Reading View**, and **Slide Show** views.

8 Scroll the summary area as needed to view all the slides

Presenter View

1 Select the **Slide Show** tab, and check the box to enable the **Use Presenter View** option

If your system has dual-monitor support you can run your presentation from one monitor, while your audience views it on a second monitor (or on a projector screen).

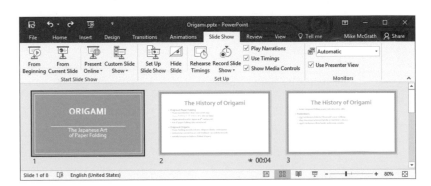

2 If you have attached a second monitor, launch Windows' **Control Panel**, then choose **Adjust screen resolution**

Appearance and Personalization
Change the theme
Adjust screen resolution

3 In the Screen Resolution dialog, click the **Multiple displays** box and select **Extend these displays**

When you change your display settings, you must confirm to keep the changes within 15 seconds or the changes will automatically revert to the previous ones.

4 Click **Apply**, then click **Keep Changes** when prompted and click **OK** to enable multiple display output

5 Select the **Slide Show** tab and click **From Beginning** to run the slide show on the two monitors

The first monitor gives the presenter's view, with the current slide and its associated notes, plus a preview of the next slide. There's also a Slide bar, to change the sequence of slides during the show.

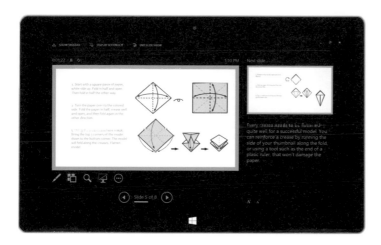

If you do not have a second monitor or projector attached, you can still select **Presenter View** and press **Alt + F5** to run the show from the presenter's view only.

The second monitor is for your audience and displays the current slides in full-screen mode.

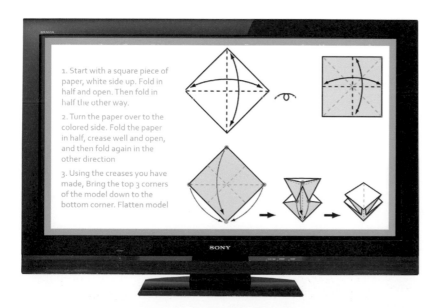

Use the **Zoom** button to enlarge the notes and make them easier to read while giving the presentation.

Choose a Template

1 In PowerPoint, select the **File** tab, then click **New** to display the example templates provided

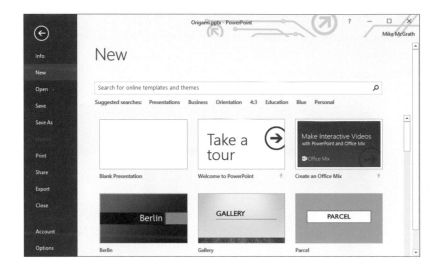

2 Select a template, for example **Slice**, to see details and view images using the themes and colors offered

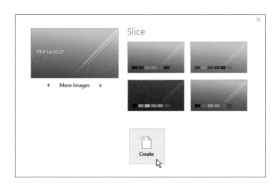

3 To make a presentation using the template, click **Create**, otherwise close the overview and review other templates

4 You can use one of the suggested categories, for example **Business**, to search for online templates and themes

Suggested searches: Presentations   **Business**   Orientation

5 PowerPoint searches online for relevant templates and themes of your selected category

6 Thumbnails and links are displayed for the items located, and the associated sub-categories are also listed

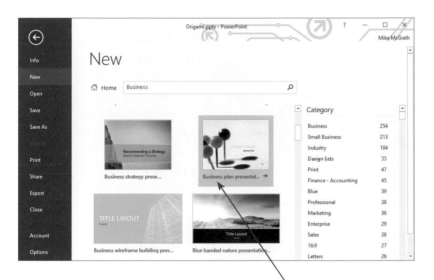

PowerPoint shows the number of templates in each sub-category, and you can select these to identify more closely a suitable template.

7 Select, for example, the **Business plan presentation**, and you'll see it consists of 12 slides on various topics

8 Click **Create** and the template will be downloaded, then a presentation based on it will be opened

The templates that you download and review will be added to the templates displayed when you select **File**, **New** in future sessions.

121

Use the Template

1 When you create a new presentation with a template, it opens showing the predefined slides and content

You can revise the text, add and replace images with your own pictures, and make your own presentation based on the template.

2 You can edit any of the slides, remove unnecessary slides or add new slides (using the same theme if desired)

3 To make it easier to reorder the slides, select the **View** tab and click **Slide Sorter**

The template will be retained in its original form in case you want to use it again in the future.

4 Save the presentation, with a new name to preserve the changes

Print the Slide Show

1 Select the **File** tab, then click the **Print** button to specify the printer and other printing options

Print Preview is provided, and you can use the scroll bar to view the slides in your presentation. The Zoom bar allows you to take a closer view.

2 Select the printer you want to use, or accept the default

3 Enter slide numbers or ranges, and the **Print All Slides** setting changes to **Custom Range**

You can choose to print the document in **Grayscale**, or **Pure Black and White**, even if the presentation itself is in full color.

4 Click the **Print Layout** button to choose the document type – you can print **Full Page Slides**, slides with **Notes Pages**, or an **Outline**

5 If you select **Handouts**, you can specify the number of slides to a page, and the order (horizontal or vertical)

6 You can also select **Frames Slides**, **Scale to Fit Paper**, and **High Quality** printing

Rehearse Timings

To establish the timings for each slide, you may need to rehearse the presentation and record the times for each step.

1 Select the **Slide Show** tab and click the **Rehearse Timings** button in the Set Up group

2 The slide show runs full-screen in manual mode, with the timer superimposed in the top left corner

3 Advance each slide or animation, allowing for viewing and narration, and the times will be recorded

4 When the presentation finishes, you can choose to keep the new slide timings for the next time you view the show

5 The view changes to **Slide Sorter,** with individual times for the slides. Make sure that **Use Timings** is selected

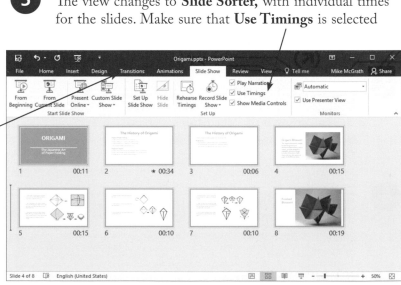

Hot tip

You can make the presentation easier to run by assigning timings to the slides, so that it can run automatically.

Hot tip

The timer shows the duration so far for the individual slide, and for the presentation as a whole.

Don't forget

Select the **Transitions** tab to make further adjustments to the times for particular slides.

Save As Options

1 Select the **File** tab and the Info view is selected, with all the details of the presentation file

Hot tip

There are several formats you can save your PowerPoint 2016 Presentation in, enabling you to share it with other users.

2 Click **Save As**, choose a location, then click the **Save as type** box, to see which file formats are supported

3 The PowerPoint Presentation (**.pptx**) format is the default, and is the file type that is designed for editing the presentation

4 Select the PowerPoint Show (**.ppsx**) format for the file type that is protected from modification. This will open in the **Slide Show** view

Don't forget

Save in the **PowerPoint 97–2003 Show** format (or **PowerPoint 97– 2003 Presentation** format), to allow users with older versions of PowerPoint to view (or modify) the presentation.

Package for CD

1 With the presentation open, select the **File** tab, **Export**, **Package Presentation for CD** and then **Package for CD**

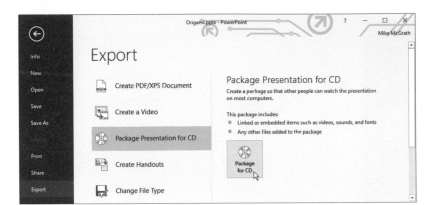

2 Type a name for the CD, then click **Copy to Folder**

3 Edit the folder name and location, if necessary, then click **OK**

4 The presentation files are added to the folder, along with all the files needed to run the PowerPoint Viewer

5 Confirm that you have everything you need, then go back to the Package for CD dialog (see step 2) and this time select **Copy to CD**. You'll be prompted to insert a blank CD, and the files will be added

7 Notes

OneNote is a great note-taking application that is easy to use, organized like a paper notebook, and is crammed with features. Here, we take a look at some of the cool and useful things you can do with OneNote.

OneNote 2016

OneNote is the digital version of a pocket notebook, giving you the means to easily capture, organize, and access all the information you need for a task or project, in any format – typed, written, audio, video or images.

The first version, OneNote 2003 was a stand-alone product. The next version, OneNote 2007, was in three of the Office 2007 editions. OneNote 2010 was in all Office 2010 editions except Starter. OneNote 2013 was in all editions of Office 2013, and OneNote 2016 is included in all editions of Office 2016.

To start using OneNote 2016 on your computer:

1 Launch the OneNote application, using any of the methods described on pages 12 and 13 – via the Start menu, taskbar icon, Search box, or ask Cortana

2 OneNote starts up and opens with the **Quick Notes** section selected, and displaying an advice page headed "OneNote: one place for all of your notes"

OneNote is also available as a free, standalone application for Windows, OS X, Windows Phone, iOS, and Android.

3 In the right-hand pane, select the page item entitled "OneNote Basics" to see the second advice page

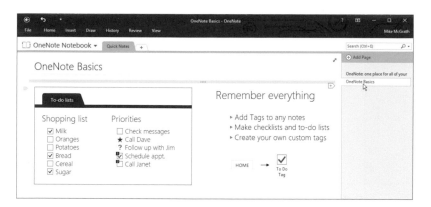

This describes the many benefits of the OneNote application:

- **Remember everything** – make checklists and to-do lists.

- **Collaborate with others** – share notes with colleagues, friends, and family via OneDrive.

- **Keep everything in sync** – store all of your notes on the cloud for access from anywhere, and on any device, via OneDrive.

- **Clip from the web** – save screenshots of any item you find of interest on any web page.

- **Organize with tables** – create data tables that can be converted later for your Excel spreadsheets.

- **Write notes on slides** – send PowerPoint slides or Word documents to OneNote.

- **Integrate with Outlook** – insert meeting details and take notes of your meetings.

- **Add Excel spreadsheets** – keep track of your finances, and budgets, or anything you want to track.

- **Brainstorm without clutter** – share only the essentials in notes to focus on the important matters.

- **Take Quick Notes** – quickly jot down thoughts and ideas as they occur to you.

The first time OneNote starts, a folder named "OneNote Notebooks" gets added to your Documents folder.

Some applications, such as Microsoft Edge, let you instantly share content to OneNote.

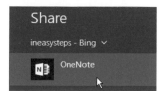

Create a Notebook

You can create a new OneNote notebook from scratch:

1 Open OneNote and select the **File** tab, then click **New**

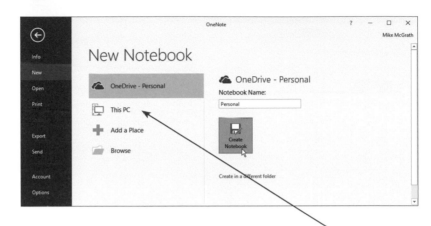

2 Choose where to put the notebook, such as in the cloud on your **OneDrive**, or locally on **This PC**

3 Type a name for your notebook into the **Notebook Name** box. For example, type "Personal", "School", or "Work"

4 Click the **Create Notebook** button to add the new notebook to your chosen location

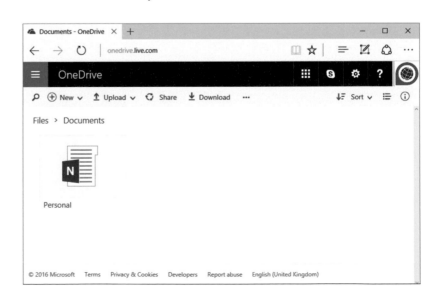

Don't forget

If you create a notebook on OneDrive you can access it from anywhere, and on any device that has a OneNote app installed – including Android devices.

5 See the new empty notebook open in OneNote on your computer, with the name you chose

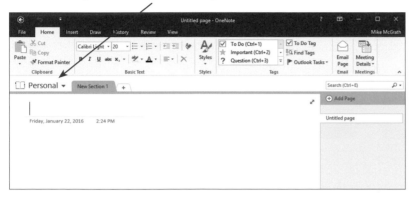

OneNote has a Ribbon that you can expand and collapse in just the same way as other Office applications, such as Word (see page 15).

6 To close the notebook, select the **File** tab, then click the **Settings** button and choose **Close**

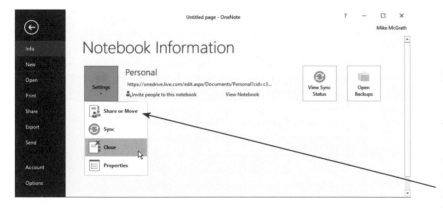

You can move a notebook from your computer to your OneDrive using the **Share or Move** option on this menu.

7 To re-open a notebook, select the **File** tab, then click the **Open** option and choose the name of your notebook. Alternatively, locate it from your documents folder on your PC

Add Sections

A OneNote notebook is arranged into sections and pages containing your actual notes. Each section can be uniquely named and colored, for easy identification, and you can add as many pages as you like to any section:

Unlike paper notebooks, a OneNote notebook will never run out of pages.

1 A new notebook is created with a section named "New Section 1" by default. To rename a section, double-click its current name, then type a new name and press **Enter**

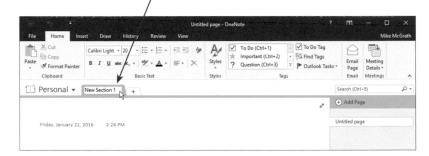

2 To add a new section, click the **+** symbol on the small tab next to the last section tab

Hot tip

To change a section color, right-click the section tab then choose **Section Color** from the menu, and pick a color.

3 Rename new sections and see they are automatically colored, to distinguish them from other sections

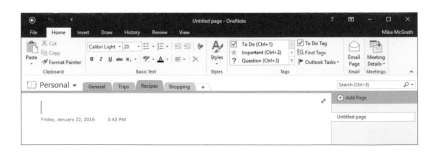

Add Pages

1 A new section is created with a blank page header by default. To rename a page, click the header area at the top of the page, then type a page title and press **Enter**

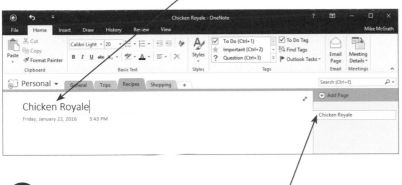

Hot tip

The date and time of the page's creation is automatically added below the header, but you can click on that date and select another date from the calendar menu that appears.

2 See the page name now appear in the pages pane, and on the OneNote window title bar

3 To add another page, click the **Add Page** button

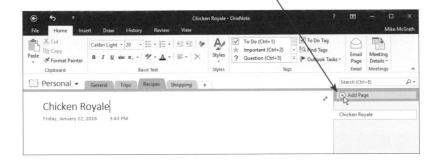

4 Rename the new page and see it also added to the pages pane

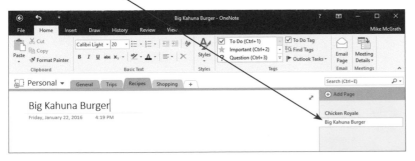

Click on any page in the pages pane to flip to that page.

Make Notes

There are many ways to create note contents in OneNote, such as typing, copying, drawing, and speaking. Additionally, devices that are touch-enabled allow you to handwrite notes, and OneNote can even convert your handwritten notes to text.

1 Open OneNote and choose a section within a notebook, then click anywhere on a page and simply start typing

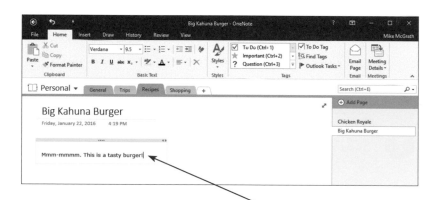

Hot tip

To handwrite notes, choose the **Draw** tab, then select a pen from the Tools group and write on the page with the mouse or touch-enabled stylus.

2 See the text you type appear within a note container box

3 Click elsewhere on the page to begin typing a new note

4 Double-click on the text in a note container to see formatting options appear

Beware

To convert handwritten notes to text, choose the **Draw** tab, then select **Ink to Text** from the Convert group. Your note now appears as text in a note container – but be sure to check the conversion for accuracy!

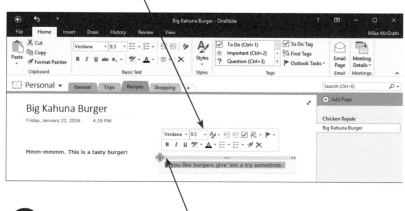

5 Click on the header bar of a note container to drag your notes around the page

6 To begin a bulleted list, type * (an asterisk) then press the Spacebar, type the item and press **Enter**

7 Add further bulleted items until your list is complete

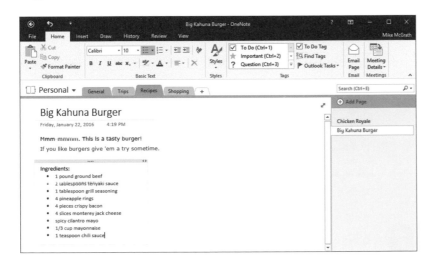

Drag the handle at the top right-hand side of a note container to make the container wider.

8 To begin a numbered list, type 1. (a number one followed by a period) then press the Spacebar

9 Type an item then press **Enter** and type the next item. Repeat this step until your list is complete

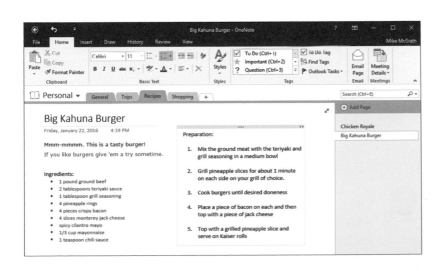

You can right-click on a note container and choose **Delete** from the context menu that appears, to remove that container from the page.

Insert Images

There are several ways to add pictures to your notes in OneNote – from an image file or screen capture on your computer, or from an online source via Bing, the cloud, or the web.

To insert an image file from your computer:

1 Select the **Insert** tab and click the **Pictures** button in the Images group, then browse to a picture on your computer

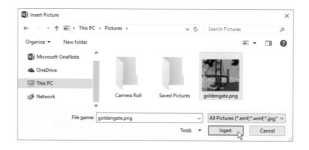

You can also choose a picture from your OneDrive account.

2 Click **Insert** to see the chosen picture appear on the current page in your OneNote notebook

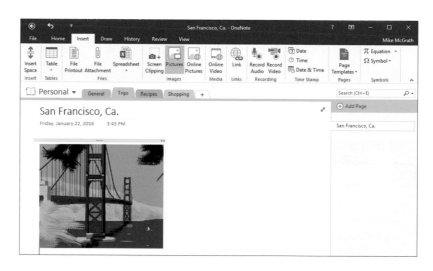

Pictures are inserted in note containers which can be adjusted with their grab handles to resize inserted images.

To insert a screen capture from your computer:

1 Open OneNote over the screen you want to capture, then select the **Insert** tab and click the **Screen Clipping** button in the Images group

2 An overlay layer appears on your screen so you can drag the cursor to select an area to clip for your notebook page

Hot tip

You can also press **WinKey + Shift + S** to clip the screen and choose a location in your OneNote notebook.

To insert an image from the web:

1 Select the **Insert** tab and click the **Online Pictures** button in the Images group, then enter a search term

2 Choose a picture, then click **Insert** to add it to your page

Hot tip

The **Online Pictures** button also lets you choose pictures from your OneDrive, or social media accounts such as Facebook or Flickr.

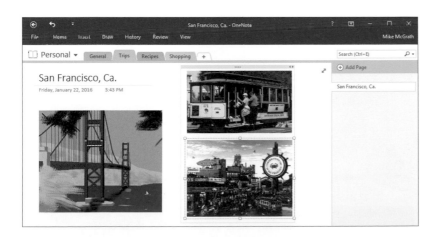

Capture Snippets

As you browse the internet you can save links to interesting snippets, or websites of interest, on a page in your OneNote notebook – so you can easily revisit that location later.

1 Select the page in your notebook where you want to add a link, then from the **Insert** tab, click the **Link** button, in the Links group, to open the Link dialog box

2 Enter the **Text to display** on your link, then type or paste the URL **Address** of the target location

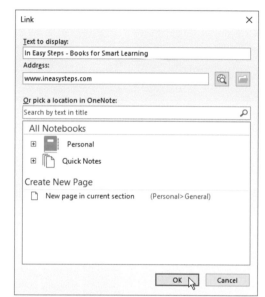

3 Click the **OK** button to see the link appear in your notebook

4 Click the link to open the target in your browser

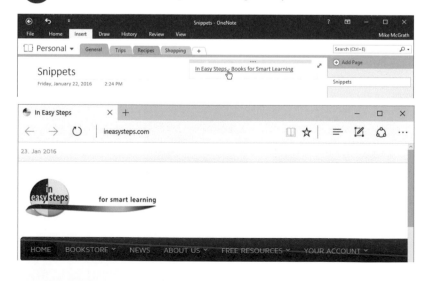

You can click the magnifying glass icon in the **Or pick a location in OneNote** box to choose another page in your notebook as the target location of a link.

You can right-click on a link in your notebook and choose **Edit Link** from the context menu, to reopen the Link dialog and modify the link.

OneNote has the ability to read text in an image using Optical Character Recognition (OCR). This allows you to easily extract text from an image and paste it into a note container anywhere in your notebook.

1 Insert an image containing text into a page in your OneNote notebook, as described on page 136

2 Right-click on the image and choose the option to **Copy Text from Picture** from the context menu

Hot tip

For best results with OCR, choose an image whose text clearly contrasts with its background picture.

3 Position the cursor on an empty part of the page, then right-click and choose a **Paste** option from the context menu

4 When the OCR feature has been successful, you will see an exact copy of the image's text appear as regular text in a note container

Beware

Like most OCR software, the OneNote character recognition is not always totally successful – be sure to check the results for accuracy.

Create Tables

OneNote provides two easy ways to add tables to your notebook pages, using keyboard shortcuts and the Ribbon.

To create a table using only the keyboard:

1 Click an empty part of the page then press the **Tab** key to create a table column

2 Type text, as content for the first column cell (heading), then press **Tab** again to create another column

3 Repeat to create more columns, then press **Enter** in the last cell on a row to create a new row

4 Repeat to fill all cells in columns and rows required

5 Press **Enter** in the first cell of a row to complete the table

Hot tip

Cells will automatically expand to fit the content as you type.

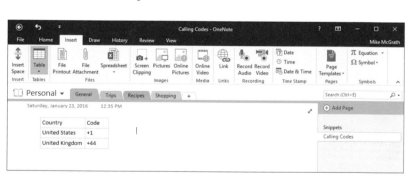

Don't forget

You can drag the vertical borders between columns to adjust each column width.

To create a table using the Ribbon:

1 Select the **Insert** tab, then click the **Table** button

2 Move the cursor over the grid, then click to select the desired table size

3 See the table inserted in your page and the **Table Tools**, **Layout** tab appear where you can change the table properties

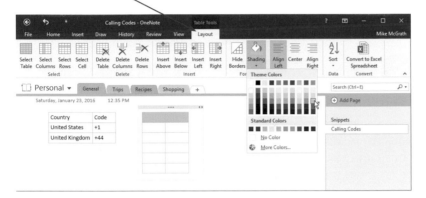

Right-click on any table and choose the **Table** item from the context menu to also find the Layout options.

4 Add text to the cells to complete the table data

You can use the **Convert to Excel Spreadsheet** button to export a table to the Excel app.

5 To sort a column into alphabetical order, click anywhere in the column to select it, then click **Sort**, **Sort Ascending**

Record Audio

OneNote is much more than a conventional notebook in which you can save text and pictures, as OneNote also lets you save audio and video recordings as notes too.

1 Connect a microphone, or check your microphone is on, then open OneNote and select the **Insert** tab

2 Prepare your message, then click the **Record Audio** button and speak your message into the microphone

Hot tip

Video message notes are created in a similar manner. Just connect a camera, or turn your webcam on, and choose **Record Video** to begin.

3 See the **Audio & Video, Recording** tab appear, then click the **Stop** button when you finish your audio note message

Beware

Don't forget to **Stop** recording when you finish speaking, or you will not be able to record another audio note.

4 Select an audio note to see the **Audio & Video, Playback** tab appear, then click the **Play** button to hear the message

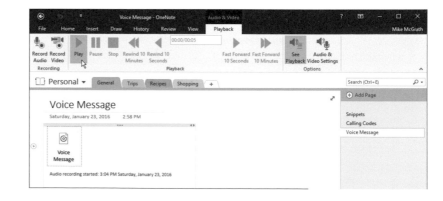

Use Templates

As with most Office applications, you may find it easier and more instructive to start from a suitable template.

1 Select the **Insert** tab, then click the **Page Templates** button in the Pages group and choose the **Page Templates** item to open a "Templates" pane

2 Expand any category in the Templates pane to discover available templates, e.g. expand the **Planners** category

3 Now, select any available template to add a page in OneNote, for example choose **Simple To Do List**

Notice the link here to find more **Templates on Office.com**.

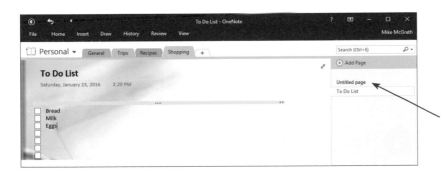

You can right-click the **Untitled page** and choose **Delete** if it's not required.

4 Click the [**X**] button on the "Templates" pane to close the pane, then rename the template list and add list items

Quick Notes

In addition to storing all your notes on pages in a notebook, OneNote can be used to quickly jot down thoughts and ideas as "Quick Notes" – even without launching the OneNote app. This feature resembles the "Sticky Notes" facility, which has been around in Windows for a while. Each Quick Note appears on your screen, like a Sticky Note, but a Quick Note is also saved in your OneNote notebook.

Beware

To use the Quick Note feature in OneNote, select **File**, **Options**, **Display** then check the box to **Place OneNote icon in the notification area of the taskbar**.

1 Press **WinKey + N** to open a small Quick Note window, then type your note text

Don't forget

Select text in the Quick Note window to see the mini toolbar, from where you can apply formatting.

2 Click the Quick Note window titlebar to see the Ribbon, if you wish to format the note or add images

3 Select the Ribbon's **View** tab, then click **Always on top** to see your Quick Note message window hover over other windows while you work

4 Launch OneNote, then click the down-arrow beside your notebook name to see the notebook list menu

5 Select the **Quick Notes** item to see your Quick Note saved in OneNote

Hot tip

You can leave your Quick Notes here if you like, or move them elsewhere.

(8) Email

The first time you use Outlook, you may need to specify your email account. Then, you can receive messages, save attachments, print messages, issue replies, and update your address book, while also protecting yourself from spam messages that might be targeted at your account. You can add a standard signature note to your messages, and subscribe to RSS feeds.

Starting Outlook

The Microsoft Outlook program provides the email and time management functions in Office 2016. To start the application:

1 Launch the Outlook 2016 application, using any of the methods described on pages 12 and 13 – via the Start menu, taskbar icon, Search box, or ask Cortana

Outlook 2016 is found in all editions of Office 2016 except for the Office 2016 Home and Student edition.

The first time you start Outlook, it helps you to define the email accounts you want to manage using this application.

2 Click **Next** to get started, select **Yes** to set up Outlook to connect an email account, then click **Next** again

3 Type your name, your email address, and your password and click **Next** to set up your account automatically

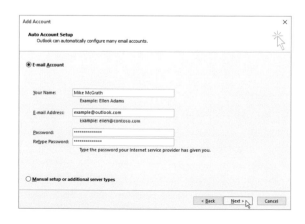

4 The wizard establishes the network connection, and searches for the server settings that support your email account

5 When your account has been located, the wizard then asks you to enter your password for that account

Outlook detects when no accounts are defined, and runs the Startup wizard to obtain details of your email account.

6 Finally, the wizard logs on to your account on the server and you can click **Finish** to see your email account is ready for use

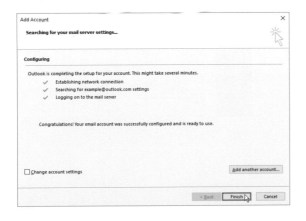

You could manually configure your account, but the easiest way to add the account is to let the wizard establish the settings for you.

Your First Messages

Outlook opens with the Inbox, showing your first email messages,
e.g. a welcome message from the ISP, or from the Outlook team.

Quick Access Toolbar   Tab bar   Tell Me Help

Ribbon

Collapse/
Expand button

Navigation   Folder   Folder   Reading
menu   pane   contents   pane

You can click the button at the top right of the Folder pane to
collapse (or expand) that pane, to provide more space to display
more message content, or to cope with a smaller screen size:

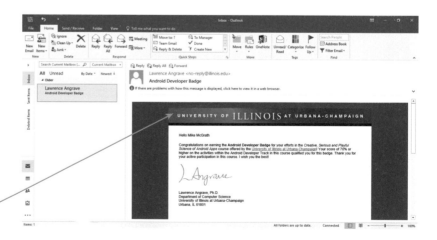

Hot tip

Outlook may prevent
the automatic download
of some pictures in the
message. If you trust
the source, you can
choose to download the
pictures.

🛈 Click here to download pictures.

For example, we trust
UIUC so opted to allow
download of the banner
graphic in this message.

Turn Off Reading Pane

1 Select **View**, **Reading Pane**, and choose **Off**, rather than **Right** or **Bottom**

2 Messages will be left unread until opened and displayed in a list grouped by either "Today" or "Older", for easy recognition

You can choose to position the **Reading Pane** below the message or hide it altogether.

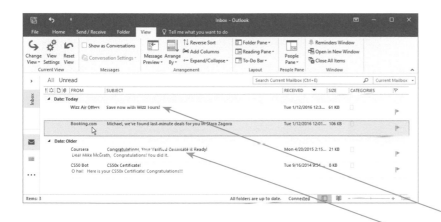

Unread messages appear in a bold, colored font. Messages that have been opened appear in a regular font.

3 Double-click on any message (or select any message and press **Enter**) to open the message and display its contents

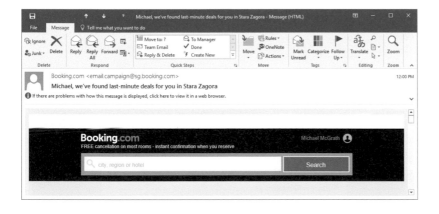

Simply reading an email message could release harmful software into your system. Turn off the **Reading Pane** and review the message first to avoid potential problems with spam and phishing emails (see pages 158-159).

4 Select **File** and then **Close** from the action list in the Backstage view to close the message window, or just click the window's **[X]** close button

Request a Newsletter

To begin exchanging messages, you'll need to share your email address with friends, contacts, and organizations. You can also use your email address to request newsletters. For example:

1 Visit the website **thrillerwriters.org** and select the link to "ITW, The Big Thrill" to see details of their free subscription newsletter

2 Scroll down to locate the form where you can apply for a newsletter subscription

3 Enter your **Email Address**, **First Name**, and **Last Name** into the input boxes, then click the **Subscribe** button

4 An invitation is sent to your email address, and a notice appears requesting email confirmation of your application

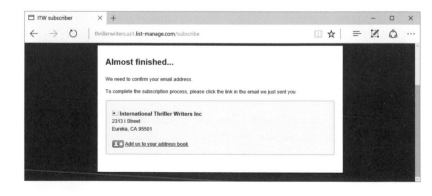

5 Open the email request message when it arrives and click the link provided, to confirm you want to subscribe

Your address could be provided, accidently or deliberately, without your permission, so you must explicitly confirm you wish to subscribe.

6 The website acknowledges your confirmation and another email is sent to your Inbox, completing the subscription

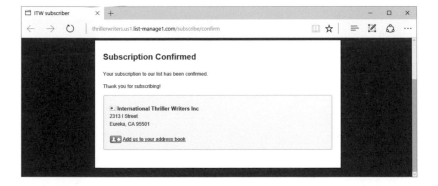

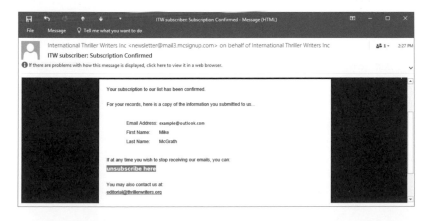

Retain this email, since it provides the links needed to change your details, or to unsubscribe, if you no longer wish to receive the newsletter.

Receive a Message

To check for any mail that may be waiting:

1 Open Outlook, select the **Send/Receive** tab, and click **Send/Receive All Folders**

2 New mail will be downloaded and displayed in the Inbox

Hot tip

Select the **Send/ Receive** tab to get extra functions that give more control over the Send/ Receive process.

3 Double-click the message title to display the contents

Don't forget

Depending on the settings, Outlook may automatically issue a Send/Receive when it starts up, and at intervals thereafter. You can also manually check for messages at any time.

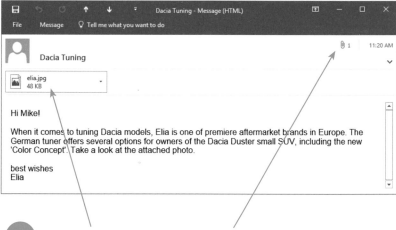

4 An icon and number by the paperclip indicates that this message has one attachment

5 Click the arrow button next to the icon to open a drop-down menu offering choices for how to treat the attachment

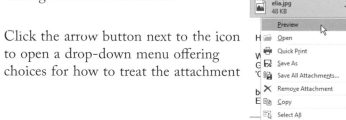

...cont'd

6 Click the **Preview** option (see image in Step 5) to view the attachment without opening another program on your computer

You can choose the **Open** option to open the attachment with the program associated with the attachment's file type, such as the **Paint** program for an image.

7 Click the **Back to message** button to close the preview, then close the message window to return to Outlook

8 Right-click on a message to open a context menu, offering choices for how to treat that message. For example, choose **Delete** to send it to the Deleted Items folder, or choose **Move** and select a folder to move the message to

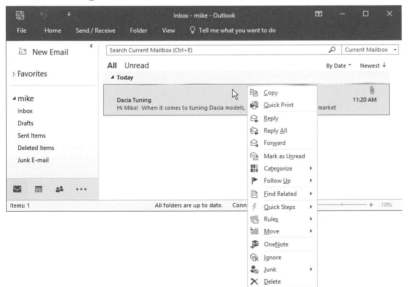

Email attachments can contain malicious software. Always be suspicious of attachments to messages from unknown sources.

Save All Attachments

To save all the attachments at once:

1 Open the message, right-click on any attachment icon and select the **Save All Attachments...** option

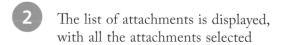
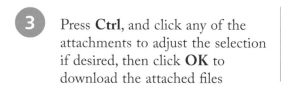

This is the safest way to handle attachments, which can then be scanned by your antivirus checker before further processing.

2 The list of attachments is displayed, with all the attachments selected

3 Press **Ctrl**, and click any of the attachments to adjust the selection if desired, then click **OK** to download the attached files

4 Locate the folder to receive the downloads (or click **New Folder** to create a new folder), then click **OK** to save

Copies of the attachment will be retained in your Inbox, until you delete the associated message (and empty the Deleted Items folder).

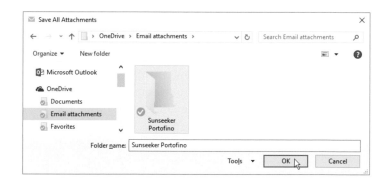

5 Open the target folder in File Explorer to view the files that you have just saved

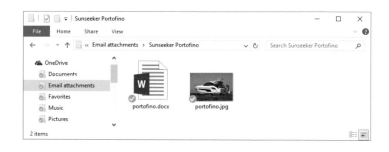

Print the Message

1 From the message, select the **File** tab, then click **Print**

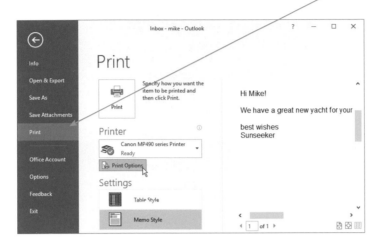

The print preview shows how the message will appear on the page. Right-click on a message and select **Quick Print** to send the message to the printer, using all the default settings.

2 Click **Print Options** to change the printer or adjust the print settings, e.g. the number of copies you want

3 Check the **Print attached files** box if you also want to print any attachments

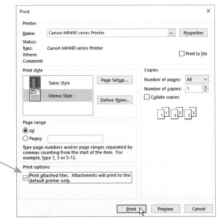

4 For picture attachments, you can choose the print size of the image

Each attachment will print as a separate print job, destined for the default printer. You can change the print size on each job, but you cannot combine the prints onto the same sheet.

Reply to the Message

1 When you want to reply to a message that you've opened, click the **Reply** button in the Respond group on the **Message** tab

2 The message form opens with the email address, the subject entered, and the cursor in the message area, ready for you to type your comments above the original text

3 Complete your response and then click the **Send** button to transfer the response – initially to the Outbox folder, and then to the Sent folder upon completion

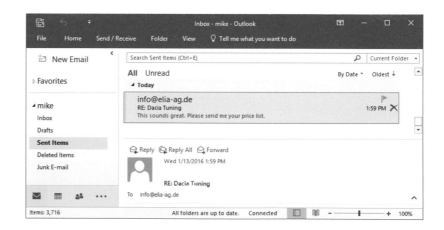

Hot tip

Click **Reply to All** to reply to multiple addressees, or click **Forward** if you want to share the message with another person.

Beware

The Reading Pane may be active in the Sent folder even if switched off in the Inbox, as it is configured individually for each folder.

Hot tip

Messages to which you have replied are marked with the date and time of your reply.

ℹ️ You replied to this message on 1/13/2016 1:59 PM.

Add Address to Contacts

Whenever you receive an email, you can add the email address of the sender (and any other addressees) to your Outlook Contacts list.

1 Right-click the email address and select **Add to Outlook Contacts**

2 Review the data that's pre-entered, and include any extra pieces of information that you may have

3 Click **Save** to record the details in the Contacts list

4 Select the People button to open your Contacts list

You can record a large amount of information, personal or business, within the entries in the Contacts record.

157

5 Review the new addition to your Contacts list and click the **Edit** button to add further details if required

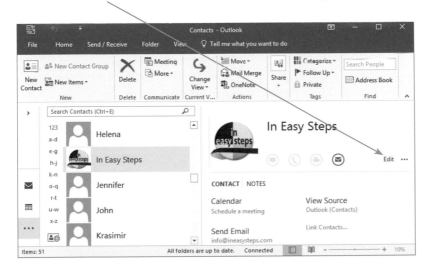

Select the Mail button to return to the Outlook email list.

Spam and Phishing

As useful as email can be, it does have problem areas. Because it is so cheap and easy to use, the criminally inclined take advantage of email for their own profit. They send out thousands of spam (junk email) messages, in the hope of getting one or two replies.

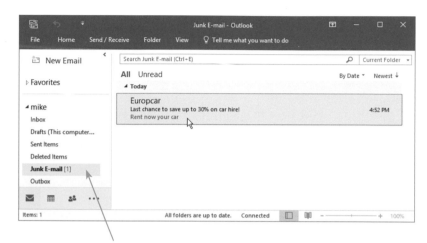

The Outlook Junk Email filter identifies spam as messages are received, and moves the invalid messages to the **Junk E-mail** folder. To adjust the settings:

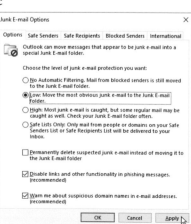

1. From the **Home** tab, select the **Junk** button in the Delete group, then click **Junk E-mail Options...**

2. Select your desired level of protection: **No Automatic Filtering**, **Low** (default), **High** or **Safe Lists Only**

3. Click the appropriate tab to specify lists of **Safe Senders**, **Safe Recipients**, **Blocked Senders**, or **International** domains

Don't respond in any way to messages that you think may be spam. Even clicking on an **Unsubscribe** link will confirm that your address is a genuine email account, and this may get it added to lists of validated account names.

Any message sent to the **Junk E-mail** folder is converted to plain-text format, and all links are disabled. In addition, the **Reply** and **Reply All** functions are disabled.

You can block messages from specified top level domain codes, and messages written in particular foreign languages.

Outlook also provides protection from messages in the Inbox:

- Links to pictures on the sender's website may be blocked, links to websites may be disabled, and you may not be allowed to use the **Reply** and **Reply All** functions.

- To explore how Outlook handles potentially damaging messages, visit the website **emailsecuritycheck.net** Submit an email address, and respond to the confirming email.

- Review the subsequent emails you receive from this website to see how Outlook responds to the various scenarios. For example, Outlook blocks access to an attachment that's executable and so potentially dangerous.

Hot tip

Links to pictures and other content from a website may be blocked, since these are sometimes the source of viruses and other threats. Only download them if you trust the sender.

Beware

Some spam messages and websites try to trick you into providing passwords, PINs, and personal details. Known as phishing (pronounced "fishing") they appear to be from well-known organizations such as banks, credit cards, and charities.

Don't forget

The attachments and links in these test emails are innocuous, but do illustrate ways in which the security of your system could be impacted.

Create a Message

1 Select the **Home** tab and click the **New Email** button to open a mail message form

Hot tip

You can also select **New Email Message** from the Jump list, which appears when you right-click the program entry on the taskbar (or right-click the Outlook program entry on the Start menu).

2 Click the **To** button to open the address book and list your contacts

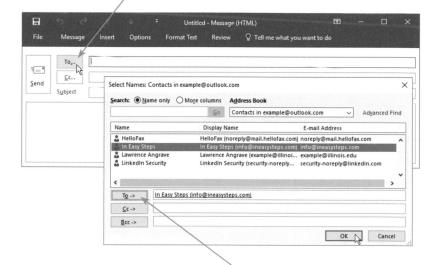

Don't forget

You can send the same message to more than one addressee. You can also select addressees for the **Cc** (courtesy copy) or **Bcc** (blind courtesy copy) options.

3 Select the addressee and click **To**, then add any other addressees and then click **OK**

4 Type the subject, greeting, and text for your message

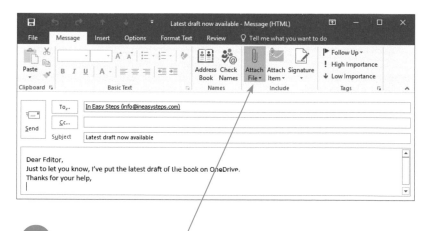

NEW

The **Attach File** button now provides a **Recent Items** list so you can quickly select recent documents to attach to a message.

5 If required, click **Attach File** and select any files to attach

Insert a Signature

You can create a standard signature to add to the emails you send.

1 Select the **Insert** tab and click **Signature** in the Include group, then click **Signatures**

2 Click the **New** button to open the New Signature dialog, then specify a name for the signature and click **OK**

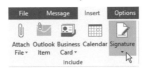

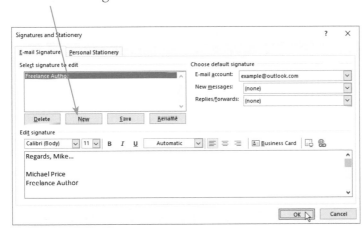

Hot tip

The first time you select the **Signature** button, there'll be no signatures defined, so you must start off by creating one.

3 Add the signature text and click **OK** to save it by name

4 Position the typing cursor where you want to insert a signature, then click **Signature** again and select the name of the signature you want to insert

Don't forget

You can specify one of your signatures as the default for new messages, or for replies and forwards, and the appropriate signature will be automatically applied to future messages.

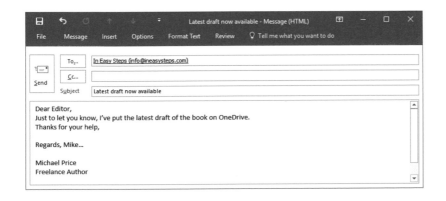

161

Don't forget

Click the **Send** button to store the message in the Outbox (if you are offline), ready for the next Send. Click the **Send/Receive** tab and select **Send/Receive** to send immediately.

Message Tags

You can use tags to help sort and organize messages.

1 Select a message, then select the **Home** tab

2 Click **Unread/Read** to toggle the read status of the selected message

3 Click **Categorize** to choose a color to associate with the selected message

Beware

Email accounts that use an IMAP connection do not have the **Categorize** tag for their messages.

4 The first time you select a specific color, you'll be asked if you want to rename it, or assign it a shortcut key

5 The **CATEGORIES** column is added to the Inbox view, and this can also be used to order the messages

Hot tip

Flagged messages are automatically added to your **Task** list.

6 Click the **Follow Up** button on the Home tab to assign a reminder flag to the selected message

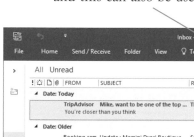

RSS Feeds

RSS (Rich Site Summary/Really Simple Syndication) is a way for content publishers to make news, blogs, and other information available to their subscribers, using a standardized XML format that can be viewed by many programs. You can add RSS "feeds" and view subscriptions in the Outlook application.

1 When you find an RSS feed you would like to subscribe to on a website, you need to copy the feed URL address

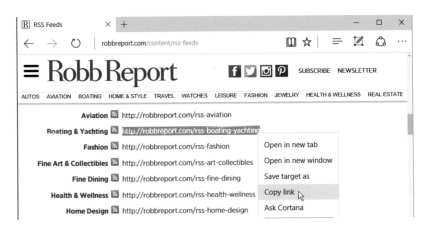

You can subscribe to RSS Feeds in some web browsers, but at the time of writing RSS Feeds are not supported by the Microsoft Edge browser.

163

2 In Outlook, select the **Folders** view

3 Right-click on the **RSS Feeds** folder, to open its context menu, then choose to **Add a New RSS Feed...**

4 Position the typing cursor in the location box, then press **Ctrl + V** to paste in the copied URL, then click **Add**

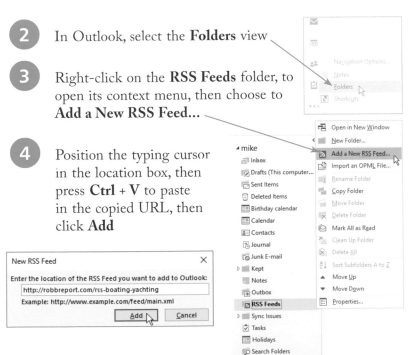

When you subscribe to an RSS Feed it adds its own folder within the **RSS Feeds** folder.

Hot tip

When you subscribe to RSS feeds from a web browser, you can use Outlook to view the updates as they arrive.

5 A dialog asks you to confirm whether you want to add the feed – click the **Advanced** button

6 Enter an RSS **Feed Name** and select any required configuration changes, then click **OK** to close the options

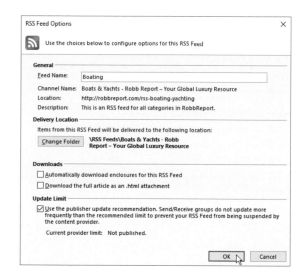

Don't forget

To ensure that the feeds remain synchronized, select **File**, **Options**, **Advanced**, and then check the option to **Synchronize RSS Feeds**.

7 Now click **Yes** to confirm you want to add the feed, and see the feed items appear in Outlook

9 Time Management

Outlook is much more than an email manager. It is a complete personal information management system, with full diary and calendar facilities. It enables you to keep track of appointments and meetings, and to control and schedule your tasks. You can keep notes, make journal entries, and correlate all these with email messages relating to those records.

Outlook Calendar

The Outlook Calendar handles time-based activities, including appointments, meetings, holidays, courses, and events (single-day or multi-day). It provides a high-level view by day, week or month and will give you reminders when an activity is due. To open:

1 Click the Calendar button on the Navigation bar

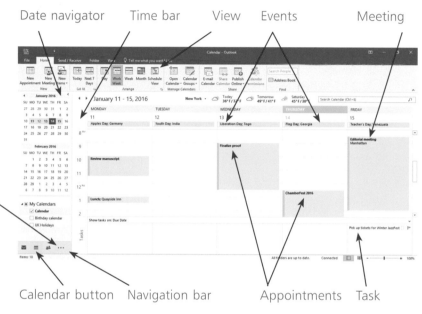

Date navigator   Time bar   View   Events   Meeting

Calendar button   Navigation bar   Appointments   Task

Hot tip

To customize the navigation bar, click the ••• ellipsis button, then select **Navigation Options** and choose your preferred options.

You can also view current calendar events on the Today page:

2 Click the Mail button, then select your email account

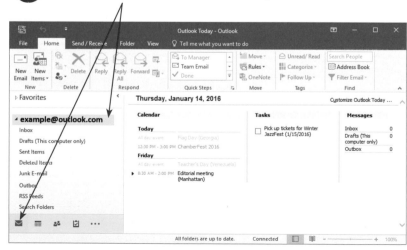

Don't forget

The Outlook Today page displays a summary of the calendar activities, the tasks, and the counts of unread messages on your system. Click the **Calendar** header to display the full calendar.

Schedule an Appointment

An appointment reserves space in your calendar for an activity that does not involve inviting other people, or reserving resources.

1 Open the Calendar (day, week or month view) and use the date navigator to select the day for the appointment

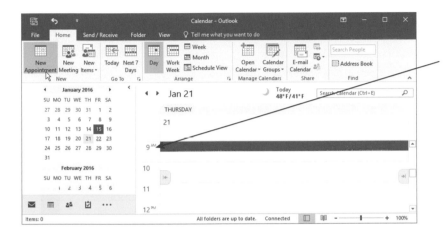

You can also double-click the hours area, or right-click that area and select **New Appointment**.

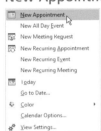

2 Using the mouse pointer select the time the appointment should begin, then click the **New Appointment** button

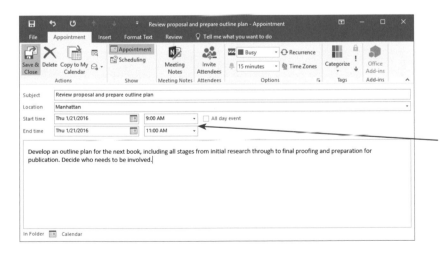

To change the **End time** and duration, click the down-arrow and select a new value. You can also change the **Start time** (the current duration will be maintained).

3 Type the **Subject**, then select the end time, enter any other details you have, such as **Location** and a description, then select the **Save & Close** button

Change Appointment Details

The appointment is added to the calendar, which shows the subject, start time, duration and location. Move the mouse over the appointment area to see more details.

1 Select the appointment and the **Calendar Tools** tab is added, with related options displayed on the Ribbon

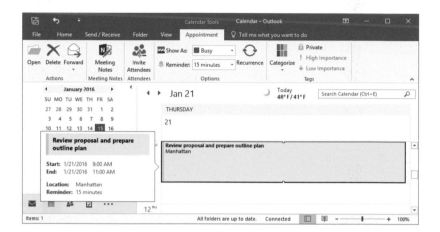

Don't forget

Single-click the calendar at the appointment area and you can edit the text of the subject title. Double-click the area and you will open the appointment for editing.

2 Click **Open** (or double-click the appointment) to open the appointment editor form (see page 167), add or change any of the details and then click **Save & Close**

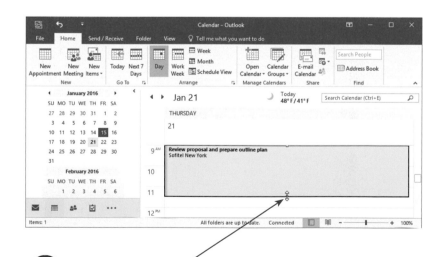

Hot tip

By default, you will get a reminder pop-up for the appointment 15 minutes before the start time, or you can set your own notice period (values between zero and two weeks), or turn off the reminder completely.

3 Drag the appointment block to change the start or finish times. The duration changes to match

Recurring Appointments

When you have an activity that's repeated on a regular basis, you can define it as a recurring appointment.

1 Open the appointments form and specify the details for the first occurrence of the activity, then click **Recurrence**

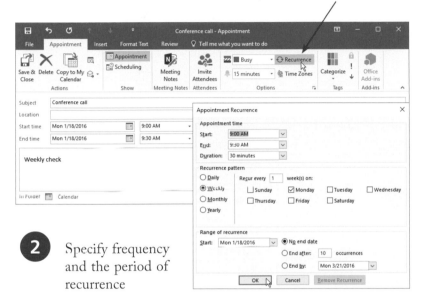

2 Specify frequency and the period of recurrence

3 Click **OK**, then click **Save & Close** to record the changes

4 All the occurrences will be displayed in the calendar

You can take an existing appointment or meeting, and click **Recurrence** to make it a recurring activity.

Unless you limit the number of recurrences, or set a termination date, the activity will be scheduled for all possible days in the future.

Depending on the view chosen and the space available, the appointment may be indicated with an icon.

Create a Meeting

1 Double-click the appointment entry in the calendar, and click the **Invite Attendees** button in the Attendees group

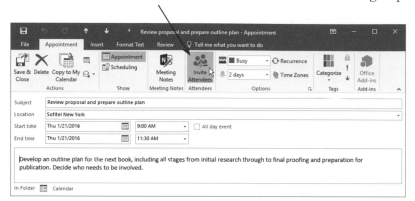

Hot tip

You can convert an existing appointment into a meeting by defining the attendees and sending invitations.

2 On the invitation message form displayed, click the **To** button to open the contacts list

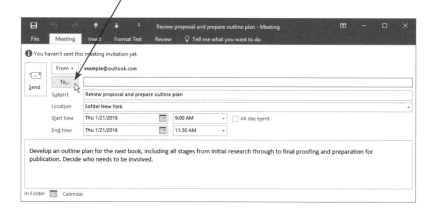

Don't forget

You can also schedule meeting resources such as rooms, screens, and projectors.

3 Select each **Required** or **Optional** attendee in turn, then click **OK**

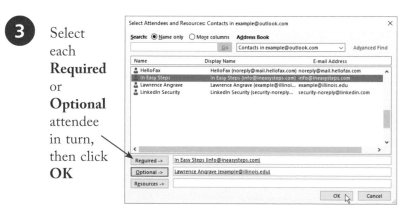

4 When all the attendees have been added, click the **Send** button to send the invitation to each of them

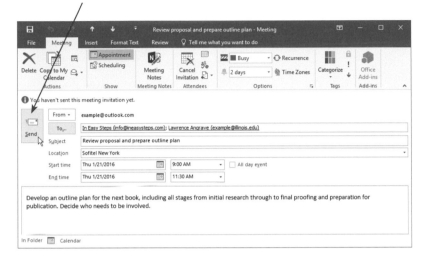

Reminders will be sent.

5 The invitation will also be received in the organizer's Inbox

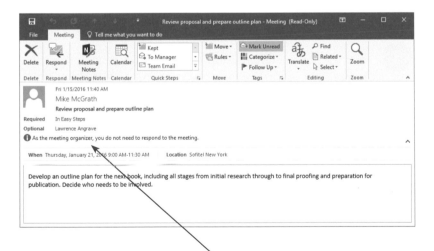

You can double-click the meeting entry in your calendar to view the current status, which will initially show no responses received.

🛈 No responses have been received for this meeting.

6 There's no response required from the organizer

Respond to an Invitation

1 When other attendees receive and open the invitation, buttons to accept, tentatively accept, or decline the invitation are provided, and they may reply with a message

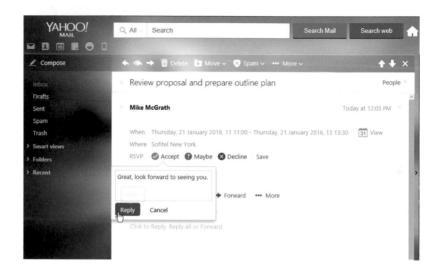

You can click the **Maybe** button to tentatively accept an invitation.

2 Click **Accept**, then add a message if desired and click **Reply** to respond to the invitation

3 The status of the invitation changes according to the response chosen – in this case its status is "Accepted"

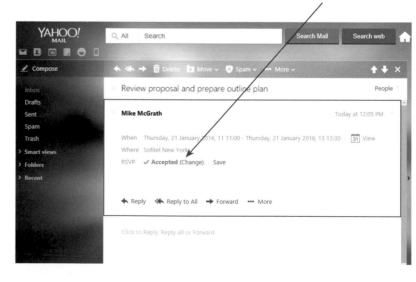

The attendees need not be using a version of Outlook in order to receive and respond to meeting invitations, but some features may work better if they are also using Outlook.

4 The originator receives responses from attendees, as emails

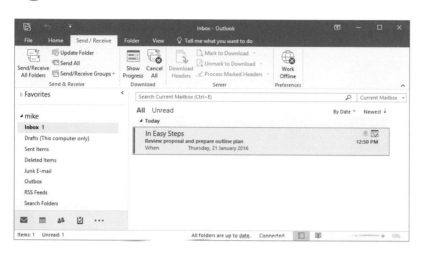

5 The message shows the attendee's response and status – in this example the invitation has been accepted

6 The meeting record also displays the updated status – indicating here that one invitation is accepted

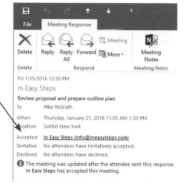

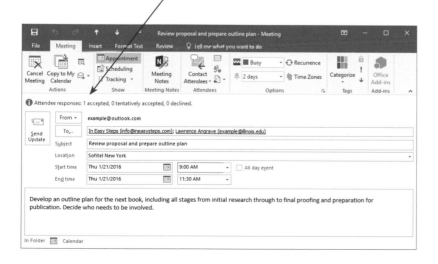

The message shows the current status, so it will show the latest information each time it is opened.

Any changes that the originator makes to the meeting details will be sent to the attendees as update messages.

Add Holidays

To make sure that your calendar is an accurate reflection of your availability, add details of national holidays and similar events:

By default, no holidays or special events are shown in your Calendar, but Outlook has a holiday file with information for 112 countries and events for the years 2012–2022.

1 Open Outlook, select **File** and then **Options**

174

Your own country or region is automatically selected each time you choose the **Add Holidays** option.

2 In Outlook Options, select **Calendar**, then click the **Add Holidays** button in the Calendar options

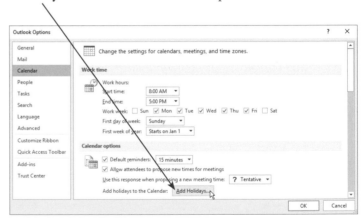

3 Select the country or countries that you wish to add, for example the United Kingdom and the United States, then click **OK**

...cont'd

4 The entries for the selected country or countries are then imported into your calendar

Hot tip

To delete holiday events later, open them in **List** view then right-click a holiday and click **Delete**.

5 Click **OK** when the holiday events have been added, then click **OK** to leave the Options

To see the new entries in the calendar:

1 Open the Calendar, select the **View** tab then click the **Change View** button

2 Now, select the **List** option

3 The calendar contents are displayed in **START** date order

Hot tip

If you have more than one country inserted, you can right-click **Location** then choose **Group By This Field**. Use this, for example, to remove the entire events for one country.

175

Report Free/Busy Time

Outlook can help you choose the most suitable times to hold meetings, based on reports from the proposed attendees, giving details of their availability.

To set up a procedure for publishing this information, each potential attendee should:

Sharing free/busy information works best on systems that use a Microsoft Exchange email server. For other systems, you may need to Import busy information (see page 177).

1 Open Outlook and select **File**, **Options**, **Calendar**

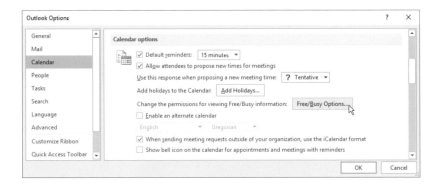

You could also set up calendars and free/busy reports to coordinate the use of resources, such as conference rooms and projector equipment.

2 Click the **Free/Busy Options** button in the Calendar Options category

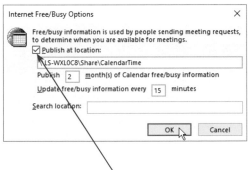

All attendees need to access the Publish at location, therefore this system works best in offices, or home networks if this feature is set up.

3 Check the box for **Publish at location**, and provide the address for a networked folder or drive that is accessible by all potential attendees, then click **OK**

The free/busy data for the specified period (e.g. 2 months) will be updated regularly (e.g. every 15 minutes). It will be stored at the location defined, in the form of **_username_.vbf** files (using the username from the attendee's email address).

Schedule a Meeting

You can use the reported free/busy information to help set up a meeting. For example, to schedule a new meeting:

1 Create the meeting with initial details (see page 170), then click 🗓️ **Scheduling** to show free/busy times

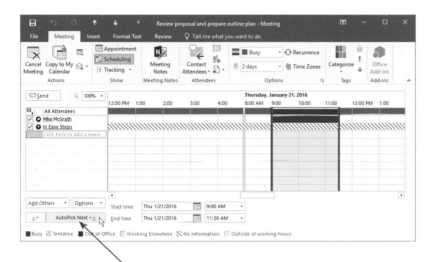

2 Click **AutoPick Next** to see next available time slots

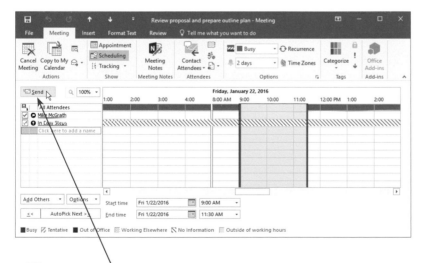

3 Click **Send** to add the revised details to your calendar, and to send an invitation (or an update) to all the attendees

You can use **Scheduling** to set up a new meeting, or to revise the timing for an existing meeting.

Free/busy reports may not be available on your system or for particular attendees. In such cases, attendees can use select **File**, **Save Calendar** to save busy times.

You can then select **File**, **Open & Export** and then **Import/ Export** to import their saved calendars and add their busy times to your calendar, ready to schedule the meeting.

⇄ Import/Export
Import or export files and settings.

Creating Tasks

To create an implicit task:

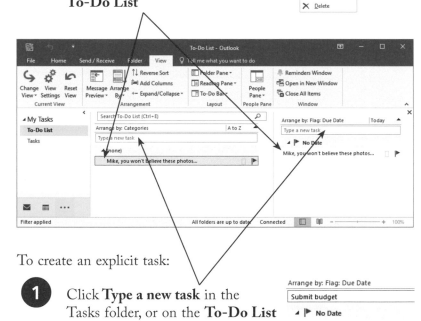

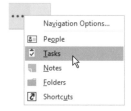

Outlook can create and manage implicit tasks as follow-ups of other Outlook items. It can also create explicit tasks, which can be assigned to others. To display the Tasks folder, click the **···** ellipsis on the Navigation bar and select **Tasks**.

1 Right-click an Outlook item (for example, a message or contact), select **Follow Up** and select the **Flag Message** option

2 The follow-up item is added to the Tasks folder, and also appears on the **To-Do List**

To create an explicit task:

This provides a quick way to generate a **To-Do List** of actions. Note that an entry changes color to red when its due date has passed.

1 Click **Type a new task** in the Tasks folder, or on the **To-Do List**

Arrange by: Flag: Due Date

Submit budget

◢ ▶ No Date

Mike, you won't believe these photos...

2 Type the subject for the task, and then press **Enter**

3 The task is inserted into the Tasks folder and **To-Do List**, with the default characteristics (the current date for the start date and the due date, and with no reminder set)

Mike, you won't believe these photos...
Submit budget

Start Date: Fri 1/15/2016
Reminder Time: None
Due Date: Fri 1/15/2016
In Folder: Tasks
Categories:

...cont'd

To make changes to the details for the task:

1 Double-click an entry on the **To-Do List**, or Tasks folder

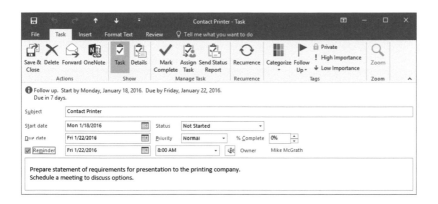

2 You can change the start date or the due date, add a description, apply a reminder, update the priority, or indicate how much has been completed

3 When you update **% Complete**, the status changes to **In Progress** or **Completed**, or you can click the down-arrow to choose an alternative

4 Click the **Details** button in the Show group to add information about carrying out the task, e.g. hours worked

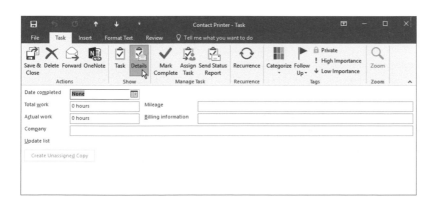

As with the editors for other Outlook items, the Tasks editor uses the Ribbon technology.

Hot tip

Click the arrows on the **% Complete** box to increase or decrease by 25% at a time, or type an exact percentage in the box.

Don't forget

Click **Save & Close** in Task or Details view, to save the changes.

Assigning Tasks

You can define a task that someone else is to perform, assign it to that person and then get status reports and updates on its progress.

To assign an existing task:

1 Open the task and click the **Assign Task** button, in the Manage Task group

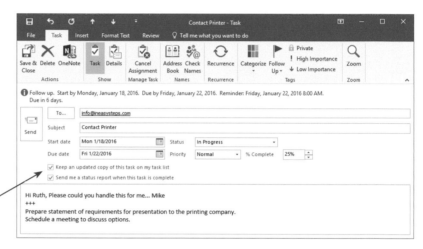

2 In the **To** box, type the name or email address for the assignee, or click the **To** button and select an entry from the Contacts list

3 Click **Send**, to initiate the task-assignment request, then click **OK** to confirm the new ownership

4 The message will be sent to the assignee, with a copy stored in the **Sent Items** folder

Accepting Task Requests

1 The task details on the originating system show that it is awaiting a response from the recipient of the task request

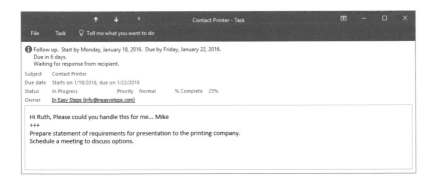

2 The task request appears in the recipient's Inbox

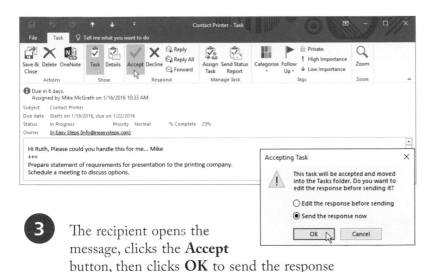

If the task request is rejected, ownership is returned to the originator, who can then assign the task to another person.

3 The recipient opens the message, clicks the **Accept** button, then clicks **OK** to send the response

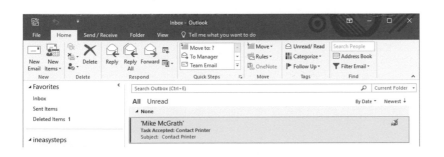

The response is sent to the originator, and a copy is saved in the **Sent Items** folder.

Confirming the Assignment

1 The response appears in the originator's Inbox, as a message from the recipient of the task request

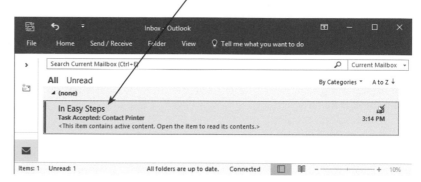

The originator is no longer able to make changes to the task details, since ownership has been transferred to the recipient.

2 When the message is opened, it shows the task with its change of ownership

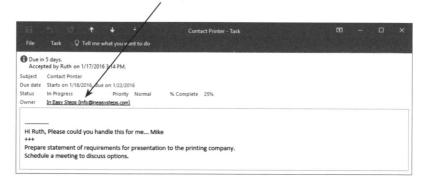

3 The task appears in the originator's Tasks folder, grouped under the new owner's name

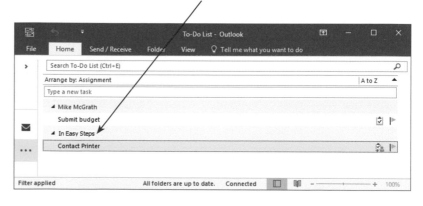

4 The new owner can change task details, and click **Save & Close** to save them, as the task progresses

5 For each change, the originator is sent an update message, to change the details of the task in the Task folder

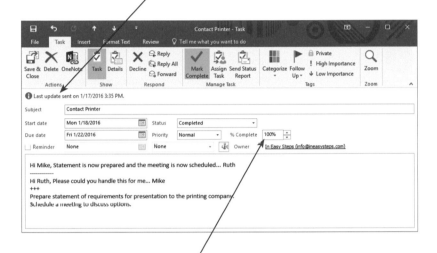

When the recipient makes any changes to the task details, messages are sent to the originator, to update the entry in their task folder.

6 When the task is marked as complete by the new owner, a final update is sent from the owner, and the task is marked as complete in the originator's task list

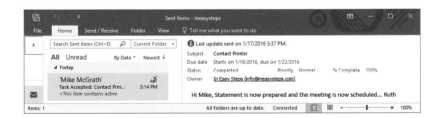

Click the message box to list all related messages in the Inbox or Sent Items folders.

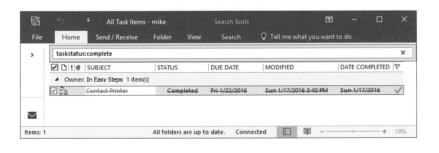

Outlook Notes

You may need a prompt, but the activity doesn't justify creating a task or an appointment. In such a case, you can use Outlook Notes. To create a note from anywhere in Outlook:

1 Click the **New Note** button on the Home tab, or press shortcut key **Ctrl + Shift + N** to start a new note

2 Type the text for your note in the form that's displayed, and it will be added to the Notes folder

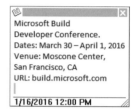

3 Click the ⋯ ellipsis on the Navigation bar and select **Notes** to see the current set of notes stored inside that folder

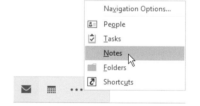

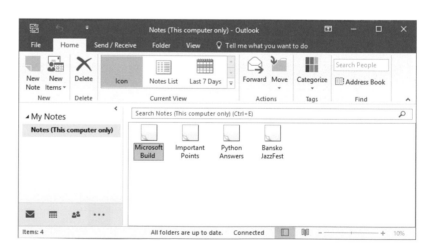

4 The note titles may be truncated, so select a note to see its full title – the text up to the first **Enter**, or else the whole text, if there's no **Enter** symbol

5 Select the **View** tab and click **List** (or **Small Icons**) to allow more space for the note titles

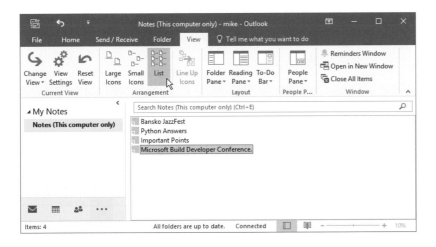

The notes are of a standard initial size, but you can click and drag an edge or a corner to make a note of any size.

6 Right-click a note to copy or print it, to forward it to another user, or to delete it

To change the view settings of your Notes folder:

1 Select the **View** tab, then click **View Settings** in the Current View group to adjust **Sort** or **Filter** options

The settings for the Icon view are shown. There'll be a different set of options available if you choose the **Notes List** or **Last 7 Days** views.

2 Click **Other Settings** to adjust the options that manage the icon placement

Journal

You can record information about activities related to Outlook items in the Journal – a type of project log book.

1 Click the ⋯ ellipsis on the Navigation bar and select **Folders**, then select **Journal** from the Folders pane – or press **Ctrl + 8**

You can select from a wide variety of Journal entry types.

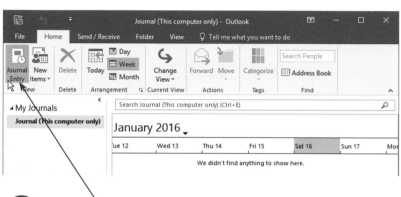

2 Select **Journal Entry** then enter your activity details

3 Click **Save & Close** to see the entry on the Timeline

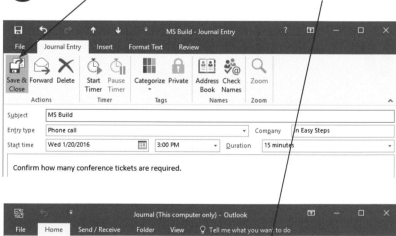

You can drag & drop items from Mail, Calendar and other Outlook folders to add them to the Journal.

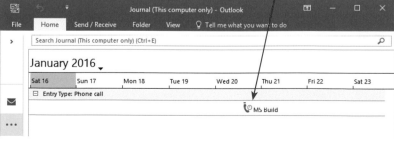

186

10 Manage Files and Fonts

It is useful to understand how Office stores and manages the files that constitute the documents and the fonts it uses, so that you can choose the appropriate formats when you share documents with other users across the internet.

Windows Versions

Microsoft has worked hard to standardize the features of Office 2016 across its various versions, although some differences exist on smaller devices due to platform and form factor limitations.

To illustrate the differences:

1 In Windows 10 on a PC or laptop, select **Start**, **All apps**, then double-click **Word 2016** to launch the Word application

2 From Word 2016 select **File** and then click **Open**

3 Choose the file location, e.g. **This PC**, **Documents**

The procedure is the same if you have Windows 10 in Tablet mode on a Touch device.

4 Select a file then click **Open** to open the document – ready for editing

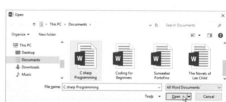

1 In Windows 10 Mobile, tap the **Word** tile to launch the Word application

2 Select a file from the Today list, or tap **Browse**

Office 2016 apps are included with Windows 10 Mobile, but if you don't see a Word tile on the Start screen, click **All apps** to find the Word item on the menu.

3 Choose a location app, e.g. tap **This Device**

4 Select a folder, then tap the check button to open that folder

5 Select a document, then tap the check button to open the selected document – ready for editing

Some functionality is omitted from the version for Windows 10 Mobile. This book uses the regular Windows 10 to demonstrate Office 2016.

Library Location

Office 2016 makes it simple to reopen a document you have saved previously in a library location, from any Office app:

1 From within an app, select **File** then choose **Open** to be presented with a variety of location options

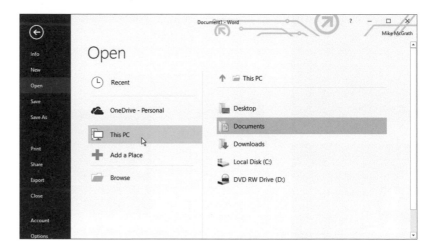

The **Add a Place** option lets you extend the list to include other locations, such as Office SharePoint for collaboration.

2 Now, choose the appropriate location of the document you want to reopen:

- **Recent** – if you have recently worked on the document

- **OneDrive** – if the document is stored on the cloud

- **This PC** – if the document is stored on your computer

Don't forget

The default location that will open from the **This PC** and **Browse** options is the Documents folder on your computer.

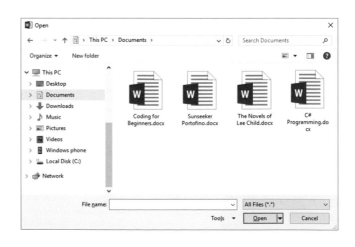

Finding Files

To reopen a document that is not stored in one of the offered top-level locations you can choose the **Browse** option to look for the document, or to search for the document by name. The search facilities are one of the strengths of Windows 10, and Office 2016 takes full advantage of them. To illustrate this, suppose you've created a document discussing the "Stayman" bridge convention, but have saved it within a sub-folder of your Documents folder.

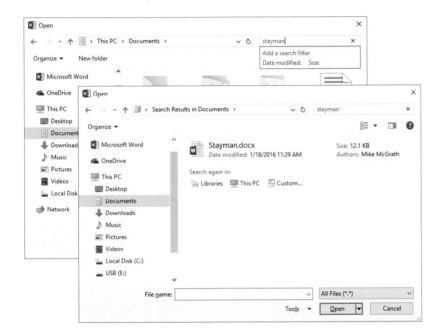

Select Documents, or choose another folder or drive where you expect to find your missing document.

To track it down when using Office 2016 with Windows 10:

1 Open Word 2016 and select **File**, **Open**, then choose the starting location, for example **Browse**, **Documents**

2 Click in the Search box, and type the search terms, for example "stayman". Matching documents from the starting location and its sub-folders are displayed

3 Right-click a file, and select **Open file location**, to see the folder where it is stored. Double-click the file to open it in Word and view or edit its contents

Any documents that contain the specified word in their titles, or in their contents, will be selected.

...cont'd

To locate documents using the operating system Search facility:

1 In Windows 10, click the Search box and simply type the search term, e.g. "stayman"

2 Matching documents, applications and other files are identified and listed so you can locate or open them

Hot tip

Click on the Search result to open that document in the appropriate Office app. Right-click on the Search result and choose **Open file location** to open File Explorer in the folder containing that document.

To locate documents directly in File Explorer:

1 In File Explorer select **This PC** then simply type the search term to automatically invoke Search

Don't forget

Although Word is used in these examples, the same search procedures apply for documents in other Office applications, for example, Excel and PowerPoint.

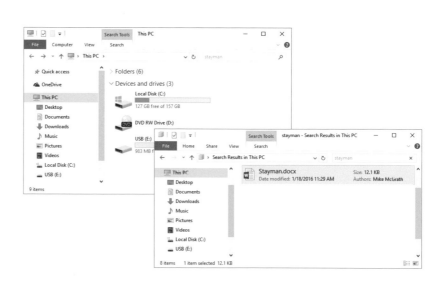

Recent Documents

When you want to return to a document that you worked with previously, you may find it in the list of recently-used documents.

1 Select **File**, **Open** then **Recent** and click an entry in the Recent list to open it

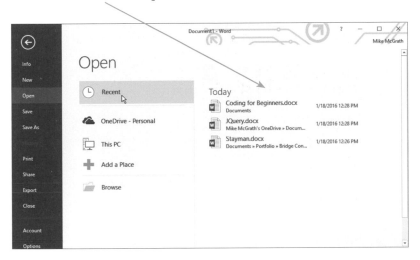

Right-click an item on the Recent list and choose **Remove from list** to remove it. Choose **Clear unpinned Documents**, to remove all the items.

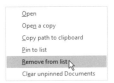

2 You can also right-click the application icon on the taskbar to display the "Jump list", which shows Recent items

Right-click on an unwanted entry on any Recent items list, and select **Remove from this list** to remove it.

3 Alternatively, right-click an application on the Start menu to see a list of its Recent items

You can also right-click a tile on the Start menu to see the Recent items list for any Office 2016 application, for example, Word, Excel, and PowerPoint.

Change File Type

To change the file types listed when you open documents:

1 From Word 2016, select the **File** tab, click **Open** and select the file location, e.g. **Documents/Misc**

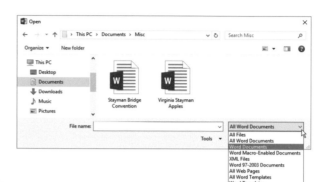

2 Choose the file type or group of types, e.g. **All Word Documents**

3 The specified file type is shown

Hot tip

Showing additional file types will make it easier to locate the correct document, when you use a variety of file types in your applications.

4 You must change folder views in File Explorer to show file name extensions for the documents (see page 22)

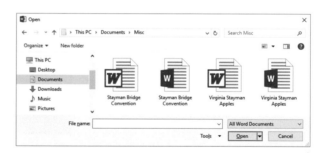

Don't forget

You can have more than one document with the same name, but with different file extensions. For example, if you have Office 2016 and Office 2003 versions.

XML File Formats

Office 2016 uses file formats based on XML, first introduced in Office 2007. They apply to Word 2016, Excel 2016, PowerPoint 2016 and Visio 2016. The XML file types include:

Application	XML file type	Extension
Word	Document	**.docx**
	Macro-enabled document	**.docm**
	Template	**.dotx**
	Macro-enabled template	**.dotm**
Excel	Workbook	**.xlsx**
	Macro-enabled workbook	**.xlsm**
	Template	**.xltx**
	Macro-enabled template	**.xltm**
	Non-XML binary workbook	**.xlsb**
	Macro-enabled add-in	**.xlam**
PowerPoint	Presentation	**.pptx**
	Macro-enabled presentation	**.pptm**
	Template	**.potx**
	Macro-enabled template	**.potm**
	Macro-enabled add-in	**.ppam**
	Show	**.ppsx**
	Macro-enabled show	**.ppsm**
Visio	Drawing	**.vsdx**
	Macro-enabled drawing	**.vsdm**
	Stencil	**.vssx**
	Macro-enabled stencil	**.vssm**
	Template	**.vstx**
	Macro-enabled template	**.vstm**

The **.docx**, **.xlsx** and **.pptx** file format extensions are also used for the Strict Open XML formats, which are ISO versions of the XML formats.

This is all handled automatically. You do not have to install any special zip utilities to open and close files in Office 2016.

The XML formats are automatically compressed, and can be up to 75% smaller, saving disk space and reducing transmission sizes and times when you send files via email or across the internet. Files are structured in a modular fashion, which keeps different data components in the file separate from each other. This allows files to be opened, even if a component within the file (for example, a chart or table) is damaged or corrupted (see page 202).

Save As PDF or XPS

There are times when you'd like to allow other users to view and print your documents, but you'd rather they didn't make changes. These could include résumés, legal documents, newsletters, or any other documents that are meant for review only. Office 2016 provides for this situation, with two built-in file formats.

Portable Document Format (PDF)

PDF is a fixed-layout file format that preserves your document formatting when the file is viewed online or printed, and the data in the file cannot be easily changed. The PDF format is also useful for documents that will be published, using commercial printing methods.

XML Paper Specification (XPS)

XPS also preserves document formatting and protects the data content. However, it is not yet widely used. The XPS format ensures that, when the file is viewed online or printed, it retains the exact format you intended, and that data in the file cannot be easily changed.

To save an Office document in either format:

Hot tip

PDF was developed, and is supported by Adobe, which provides a free Reader for viewing and printing PDF files. XPS is a competitive product from Microsoft, which also provides a free XPS viewer.

Don't forget

All the Office 2016 applications include the capability to save documents or reports in the PDF and XPS formats.

1 Open the document in the appropriate application. For example, open a Word document using Word 2016

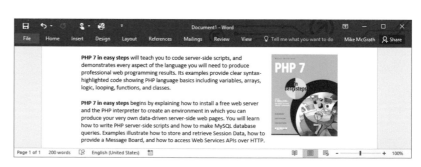

2 Make any required changes to the document, then select the **File** tab and click **Save**

3 Select the location to store the new copy. For example, choose **OneDrive** then select its **Documents** folder

4 Click the **Save as type** box, and select PDF or XPS format

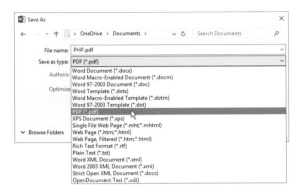

Don't forget

You can also save your documents in a variety of other formats, including ones suitable for use on web pages.

5 Select **Optimize for**, **Standard** quality, and check **Open file after publishing**, then click **Save**

Hot tip

You can choose **Minimum size** to publish the document online, for faster download times.

6 The document is saved, then displayed using your system's default application associated with the chosen format

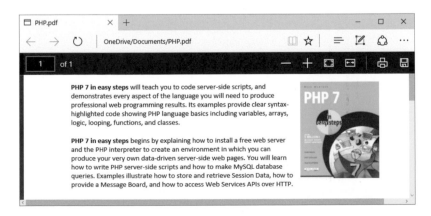

Fonts in Office 2016

There are a number of fonts provided with Office 2016 such as Calibri, Comic Sans, Gabriola, Georgia, Impact and Verdana. You can preview text using these and other Windows fonts:

 From the **Home** tab, select the text to be previewed and click the down-arrow on the Font box

Calibri is the default font for Office 2016, replacing the Times New Roman font that was the default font in earlier versions of Office.

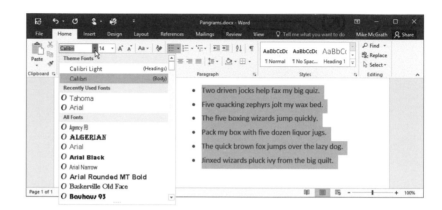

 Scroll the list to locate an interesting font, then move the mouse pointer over the font name to see an immediate preview using that font for the selected text

The font sample box usually extends over the text, hiding much of the preview. It can be dragged up to reveal more of the text, but will then display fewer fonts.

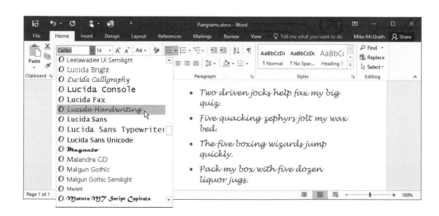

 Click on the desired font name to put the change into effect

This helps indicate how the text will appear, but it is an awkward way to explore the large number of fonts available.

...cont'd

With the help of a macro available from Microsoft, you can create a document that provides a sample of every font on your system.

1 Visit **support.microsoft.com/kb/209205**

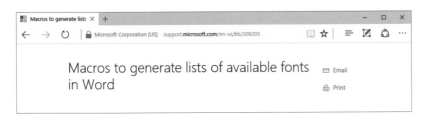

2 Scroll to **ListAllFonts,** then select and copy all of the code

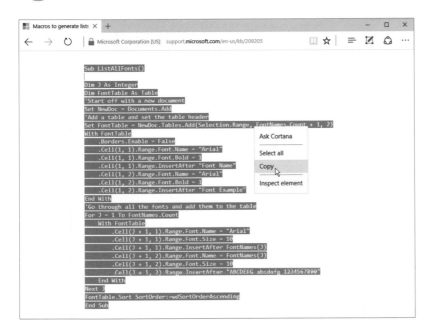

```
Sub ListAllFonts()

Dim J As Integer
Dim FontTable As Table
'Start off with a new document
Set NewDoc = Documents.Add
'Add a table and set the table header
Set FontTable = NewDoc.Tables.Add(Selection.Range, FontNames.Count + 1, 2)
With FontTable
    .Borders.Enable = False
    .Cell(1, 1).Range.Font.Name = "Arial"
    .Cell(1, 1).Range.Font.Bold = 1
    .Cell(1, 1).Range.InsertAfter "Font Name"
    .Cell(1, 2).Range.Font.Name = "Arial"
    .Cell(1, 2).Range.Font.Bold = 1
    .Cell(1, 2).Range.InsertAfter "Font Example"
End With
'Go through all the fonts and add them to the table
For J = 1 To FontNames.Count
    With FontTable
        .Cell(J + 1, 1).Range.Font.Name = "Arial"
        .Cell(J + 1, 1).Range.Font.Size = 10
        .Cell(J + 1, 1).Range.InsertAfter FontNames(J)
        .Cell(J + 1, 2).Range.Font.Name = FontNames(J)
        .Cell(J + 1, 2).Range.Font.Size = 10
        .Cell(J + 1, 2).Range.InsertAfter "ABCDEFG abcdefg 1234567890"
    End With
Next J
FontTable.Sort SortOrder:=wdSortOrderAscending
End Sub
```

3 Open a new blank document and select the **View** tab, ready to work with macros

Create and Run ListAllFonts

1 Click the arrow on the **Macros** button in the Macros group, and select the **View Macros** entry

2 Name the macro "ListAllFonts", choose **Macros in** "Document1", and click **Create**

3 Highlight the skeleton code, ready to replace it

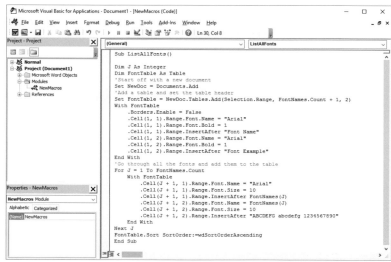

```
Sub ListAllFonts()

Dim J As Integer
Dim FontTable As Table
'Start off with a new document
Set NewDoc = Documents.Add
'Add a table and set the table header
Set FontTable = NewDoc.Tables.Add(Selection.Range, FontNames.Count + 1, 2)
With FontTable
    .Borders.Enable = False
    .Cell(1, 1).Range.Font.Name = "Arial"
    .Cell(1, 1).Range.Font.Bold = 1
    .Cell(1, 1).Range.InsertAfter "Font Name"
    .Cell(1, 2).Range.Font.Name = "Arial"
    .Cell(1, 2).Range.Font.Bold = 1
    .Cell(1, 2).Range.InsertAfter "Font Example"
End With
'Go through all the fonts and add them to the table
For J = 1 To FontNames.Count
    With FontTable
        .Cell(J + 1, 1).Range.Font.Name = "Arial"
        .Cell(J + 1, 1).Range.Font.Size = 10
        .Cell(J + 1, 1).Range.InsertAfter FontNames(J)
        .Cell(J + 1, 2).Range.Font.Name = FontNames(J)
        .Cell(J + 1, 2).Range.Font.Size = 10
        .Cell(J + 1, 2).Range.InsertAfter "ABCDEFG abcdefg 1234567890"
    End With
Next J
FontTable.Sort SortOrder:=wdSortOrderAscending
End Sub
```

4 Press **Ctrl + V** to paste the macro code copied from the Microsoft website, then select **File**, and **Close and Return to Microsoft Word**

5 Reselect **View Macros**, click the macro name "ListAllFonts", and then click **Run** to execute the macro code

6 A new document is created, displaying all font names and examples in the form of a table

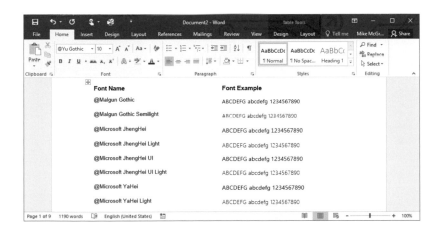

Hot tip

You can use your own text for the samples, by changing the quoted phrase in the code line: **Cell(J + 1, 2).Range. InsertAfter "ABCDEFG abcdefg 1234567890"**.

7 Save the new document, to store the table of font names and examples

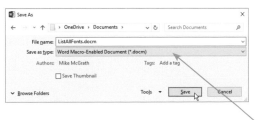

8 Also, save the first document to keep a copy of the "ListAllFonts" macro – in a macro-enabled document format

Don't forget

The macro is created in the first document, which can be closed without saving. It is not required to view the font samples in the second document. However, if you do want to save the original document, you must make it a macro-enabled document.

Document Recovery

Sometimes your system may, for one reason or another, close down before you have saved the changes to the document you were working on. The next time you start the application concerned, the Document Recovery feature will recover as much of the work you'd carried out as possible since you last saved it.

1 Open the program (e.g. Word) and click **Show Recovered Files**

If a program freezes, you may have to force Logoff, or Shutdown without being able to save your document.

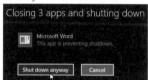

2 Check the versions of the document that are offered, and choose the one closest to your requirements

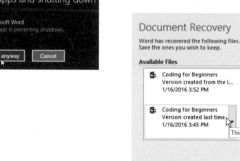

By default, documents are automatically saved every 10 minutes, but you can adjust the timing (see page 30).

3 Select **File, Save As** then rename the document if desired, and save the document

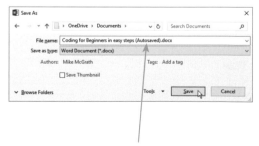

Provide a different name for the **Autosaved** version if you also want to retain the original version.

11

Up-to-Date and Secure

Microsoft Update ensures you take full advantage of Office updates. You can get the latest information and guidance, with online help. Office also provides options to enable you to protect your documents, control access to them and secure your system.

Enable Updates

The very first time you run an Office 2016 application after installation, you'll be asked to choose your preferred settings for how your Office applications should be updated in the future:

The **Use recommended settings** option will provide you with updates for Office, Windows, and other Microsoft software, together with various problem-solving facilities.

Alternatively, you can choose **No thanks** to not apply updates, though this can leave your computer open to security threats. However, you can change the update settings at a later date:

 In Windows 10, enter "settings" into the Search box, or ask Cortana to "start settings", or click **Settings** on the Start menu – to launch the system Settings screen

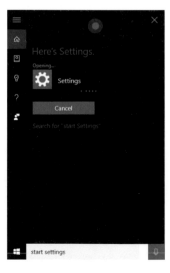

Don't forget

After you install Office 2016 and run any of the applications for the first time, you will be asked to Activate your copy of Office and then choose the settings for Update.

2 On the Settings screen, select the **Update & security** item

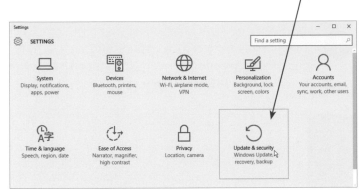

In Windows 10, you cannot find Windows Update via the Control Panel, as you could in earlier versions of Windows.

3 Next, select **Windows Update** in the left pane, then click the **Advanced options** link

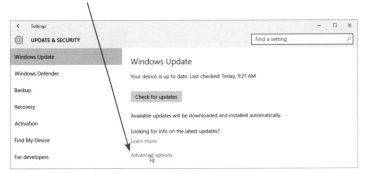

4 Now, check the **Give me updates** option to have your Office apps updated whenever your system is updated

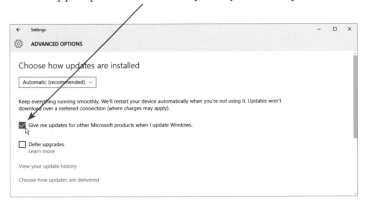

Choose the **Automatic (recommended)** option to allow Windows to automatically check for updates, and to automatically install them on your computer.

Apply Updates

If you prefer not to enable automatic updates for your Office 2016 applications, as described on the previous page, you can manually check for and apply updates at any time.

1 Launch any Office 2016 application, such as Word, then click **File**, **Account**, to see your Office **User Information** and **Product Information**

Notice that you can also configure the **Office Background** and **Office Theme** settings from the Account screen. Office 2016 provides several new themes. Try the **Dark Gray** theme for high contrast that is easy on your eyes.

2 Click the **Office Updates**, **Update Options** button to open a menu offering various settings options

3 Choose the **Update Now** option to apply all available updates immediately

Change Settings

To view updates:

1 On the **Office Updates**, **Update Options** menu, choose the **View Updates** option

2 Discover what new features have been added to your Office apps with recently applied updates

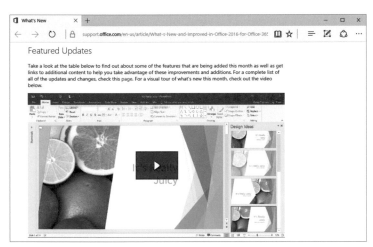

You can follow a link to the page containing a complete list of all updates and changes.

To disable updates:

1 On the **Office Updates**, **Update Options** menu, choose the **Disable Updates** option

2 Agree the User Account Control dialog to see the **Office Updates** settings change to "This product will not be updated"

You can only change Update Options if you have Administrator privileges on the system.

Office Help

If you need assistance for any Office 2016 application, you can call upon the Office Help feature – simply press the **F1** shortcut on the keyboard.

1 With an Office 2016 application open, e.g. Word 2016, press **F1** to see a Help window listing "Top categories" of help for this particular Office app

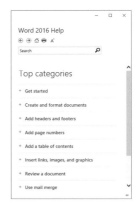

Hot tip

You invoke Office Help in the same way in each Office application, though the Help window that opens is specific to the active application, in this case, Word. The layout is similar for all the Office applications.

2 You can click on the **+** button beside any category to reveal a list of topics within that category. For example, if you are looking for help on how to add page numbers, click on **Add page numbers**

3 Choose any topic to discover help on that specific subject. For example, select **Add page numbers to a header or footer** if you want help on that specific subject

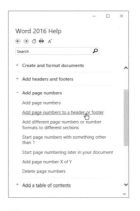

Don't forget

To use Office 2016 Help, you must have an internet connection. Unlike previous versions of Office there is no Offline Help option.

Explore Help Topics

1 You can search for assistance in a Help window by entering keywords for a subject, e.g. "word count"

Whichever topic you select, the Search box will still be accessible, so you can locate new topics or click the Home button to return to the initial Help window.

2 Click on any result topic for help on that specific subject

You can often find direct assistance by typing a query word or phrase into the **Tell me what you want to do** box on the titlebar.

1 Open a document in Word, then type "word count" into the **Tell Me** box to see an instant document analysis

The **Tell Me** box is a great new feature in Office 2016. Type in anything you like and it will attempt to help you.

Developer Tab

The Developer tab provides access to functions that are useful if you want to create or run macros, develop applications to use with Office programs, or to employ "Add-ins". It is aimed at the advanced user and for this reason, it is normally hidden.

To reveal the Developer tab in a particular Office application:

1 Open the application and select the **File** tab, then click the **Options** item to open the Options dialog

2 Select **Customize Ribbon**, then check the **Developer** box and click **OK** to close the Options dialog

Enabling the **Developer** tab for one Office application does not enable it in any of the other applications. You must enable (or disable) the **Developer** tab for each application individually.

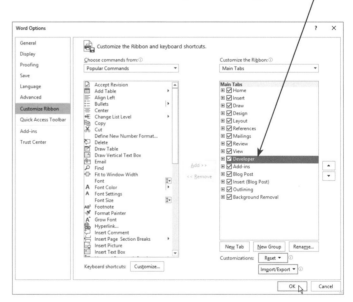

The selection of groups included in the **Developer** tab vary by application.

3 See that your Options change has been applied, and the **Developer** tab is now added to the titlebar

4 Click the **Add-ins** button to discover any extra developer features that might be useful to your document

5 Select any available Office Add-in, then click **Insert** to incorporate its functionality in the application. For example, insert **Translator** to allow language translation

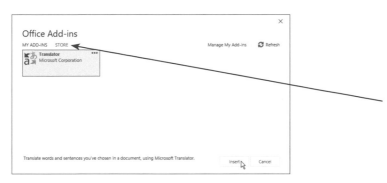

Click the **Store** link here to download Add-ins to increase available functional features.

6 See a panel appear for translations. Highlight some text in the document to select it for translation, then choose the target language. For example, choose "Spanish"

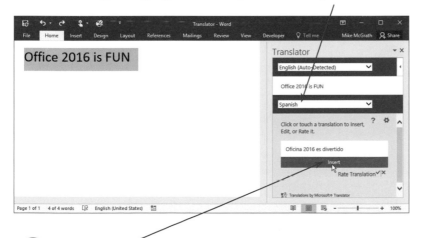

The **Translator** functionality in this example is provided by a free Microsoft Add-in, but some Add-ins in the Store need to be purchased.

7 Click **Insert** to replace the selected text with its translation

Remove Personal Information

An Office document file can contain more information than what appears when you review or print it. If the document has been subject to revision, the file may include a record of all the changes, including additions, deletions, and reviewer's comments. You may not want such information included when you publish a document, so Office 2016 makes it easy to completely remove such information from documents before publication:

1 Select the **Review** tab, and click the **Original** option – to see the document in its original form

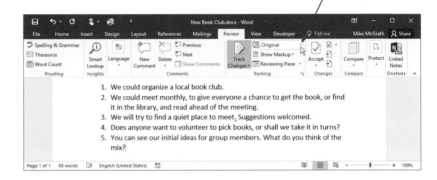

The markup includes all the changes and comments that have been applied, and may give away more information than you'd really like.

2 To see changes and comments made to the original text, click the down-arrow and select **Simple Markup**

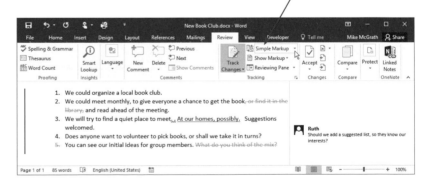

Beware

Do not make changes to your master document. It is best to work with a copy of the document, to avoid the possibility of accidently removing too much information.

3 Select **File**, **Save As**, enter a new file name then **Save** a copy document

4 Select the **File** tab, click **Info** then click the **Check for Issues** button, and select the **Inspect Document** item in the drop-down menu

You can also check for accessibility issues and compatibility issues, before making your document available.

5 Check the boxes against the document content you want to examine (or leave all items checked) then click the **Inspect** button

6 Click the **Remove All** button for each item in turn, where unwanted or unnecessary data was found

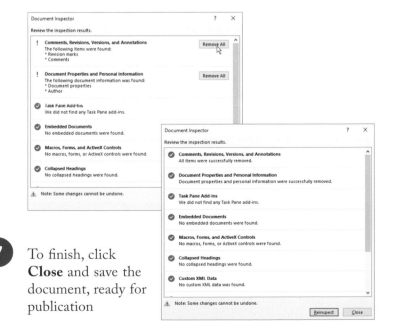

Select those elements that may contain hidden information that you want to remove. You might allow items such as headers, footers and watermarks, if detected.

7 To finish, click **Close** and save the document, ready for publication

If you've used a working copy, the information will still be available in the original document, just in case it's needed.

Protect Your Documents

When you send out a document, you might want to discourage or prevent others from making unauthorized changes to the content. At the simplest level, you could tell users that the document has been completed, and should no longer be changed.

1 Open the document, select the **File** tab, click **Info**, and then **Protect Document**, and select **Mark as Final**

Beware

Mark as Final only provides a warning to discourage users to edit the document, and there is an Edit Anyway button which dismisses this warning.

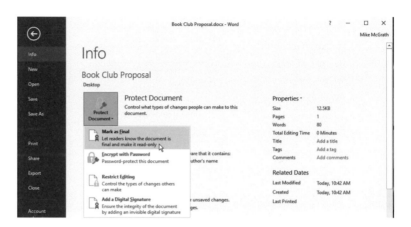

2 Click **OK** to confirm and complete the action

3 The effects of marking as final are explained

Don't forget

Another way to make the document read-only is to publish it using the PDF, or XPS document format (see page 196).

4 This is illustrated when you next open the document. You see "Read-Only" on the title bar, and a warning message

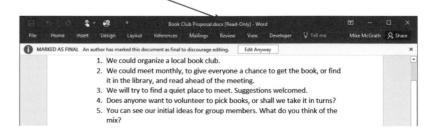

Hot tip

The Ribbon and all its commands arc hidden, and the Info page for the document confirms the new status.

Alternatively, you might choose to encrypt the document, to prohibit unauthorized changes.

1 From **Info**, **Protect Document**, select **Encrypt with Password**

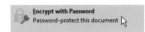

2 Provide a password for the document, click **OK**, then re-enter the password to confirm, and click **OK** again

Beware

If you lose the password, the document cannot be recovered, so you should work with a copy, and retain the original document in a secure location.

3 The contents haven't been altered, but when you close the document, you will still be prompted to save the changes

4 Now, anyone who opens the document will be required to enter the password and click **OK**

If you want to remove the encryption:

1 Open the document, then select **Encrypt with Password** again, delete the existing password and click **OK**

Don't forget

With encryption applied, no one will be able to review or change the document without the correct password, as will be indicated in the document Info page.

Restrict Permission

You can go further and apply specific levels of protection.

1 Working with a copy of your document, click **File, Info, Protect Document**, and select **Restrict Editing**

You can also click the **Review** tab and then the **Restrict Editing** button to display this pane.

2 The **Restrict Editing** pane appears, with three options

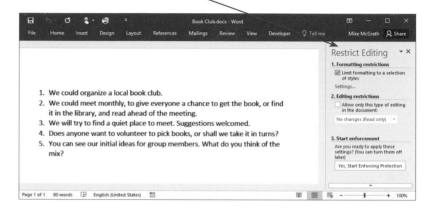

When you have selected the styles that are allowed, you can choose to remove any existing formatting or styles that would now be disallowed.

3 Choose the option to **Limit formatting to a selection of styles**

4 Click the **Settings** link, to specify styles in your document

5 Check the styles you wish to allow, then click the **OK** button to close the Formatting Restrictions dialog

6 Choose the option to **Allow only this type of editing in the document**, and select the level you will allow

7 Click the button labeled **Yes, Start Enforcing Protection** to apply your chosen restrictions

8 Enter a password twice to protect your restrictions, then click the **OK** button

9 Other users will be able to open the document for reading, but will be required to enter the password to edit the document – as permitted by your restrictions

If you want to remove the restrictions:

1 Open the document then click the **Stop Protection** button in the **Restrict Editing** pane (see Step 1 on the previous page)

2 Enter the password, then click **OK** to return the document state to become editable without restrictions

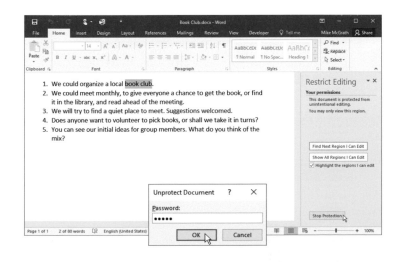

Hot tip

File, **Info** will now show that certain types of changes are restricted in this document.

Don't forget

You can give specific users permission to freely edit particular sections of the document.

Trust Center

The Trust Center contains security and privacy settings for Office applications. To open the Trust Center and display the settings:

1 Select **File**, **Options**, and then **Trust Center**

This shows opening the Trust Center from Word. It is similar for other Office applications, though the options offered may vary.

If you make changes to run macros you have created or received from a reliable source, be sure to restore the original Trust Center **Macro settings** after you close the macro-enabled document.

2 Click the **Trust Center Settings** button and choose an option. For example, choose **Macro Settings**, to see options to Disable or Enable certain macros

Click the links in the Trust Center to display information about Microsoft support, for privacy and security.

3 Select **Add-ins** to apply control over these. For example, require all **Add-ins to be signed by Trusted Publisher**

12 More Office Apps

This provides an overview of other Office applications and shows you how you can use products that integrate with Office, and use Office online with OneDrive.

Office Tools

Language Preferences

The Office 2016 setup procedure will, by default, automatically install the language version that matches your system locale, such as English (United States). You can install support to enable spell checking and grammar checking in other languages, using the Office 2016 Languages Preferences application:

1 From **Start**, **All apps**, expand the **Microsoft Office 2016 Tools** folder, then select **Office 2016 Language Preferences** to launch the app

Hot tip

You can install additional languages for your system in Windows Settings, then choose your preferred Display Language for Office with the **Language Preferences** app.

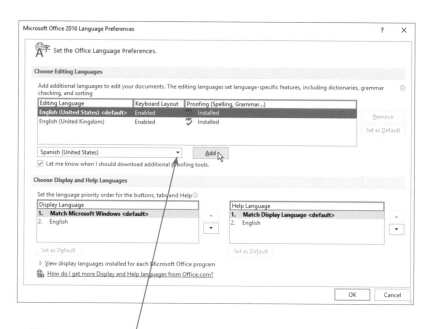

2 Click the arrow button to reveal the drop-down languages menu, and then select the language you want to install

3 Now, click the **Add** button to see the language appear in the Editing Language list

Don't forget

Notice that **Proofing** support is now added without affecting your **Keyboard Layout** setting.

Editing Language	Keyboard Layout	Proofing (Spelling, Grammar...)
English (United States) <default>	Enabled	Installed
English (United Kingdom)	Enabled	Installed
Spanish (United States)	Not enabled	Installed

Upload Center

When you save your Office documents for online storage in your OneDrive, they are first saved locally on your computer in the Office Document Cache, before being uploaded. This allows you to save changes and immediately continue working even when you are offline or have a poor network connection. You can check on the status of your online documents and manage uploads, using the Office 2016 Upload Center application:

1 Go to **Start**, **All apps**, **Microsoft Office 2016 Tools**, then select **Office 2016 Upload Center** to launch the app

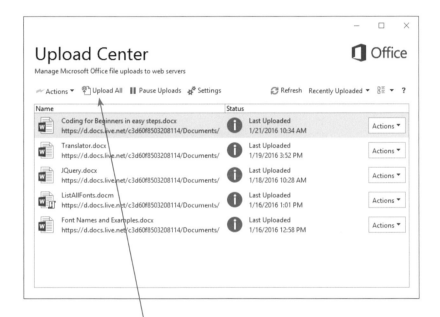

Click **Settings** to discover **Display Options** and **Cache Settings** to further manage your uploads.

221

2 Click **Upload All** to ensure the latest documents in your Office Document Cache are uploaded online

3 Select any document in the list, then click its **Actions** button for options

4 Choose the **Open Site** option to find the document in its online location

Choose the **Discard Changes** option on the Actions menu to retain the online version of the document unchanged.

Office Online

If you have a Microsoft Account and associated OneDrive, you can use the Office Online apps to create or access your Office documents from a browser, and share files and collaborate with other users online. You don't even need a copy of Office on the device that you are using:

1 Open your browser and visit **onedrive.live.com**
If you are signed in to your Microsoft Account (for example when using Windows 10) your OneDrive "Files" view appears

In OneDrive, select **New** and choose the type of Office document you want to create in the current folder, using only your web browser.

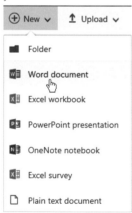

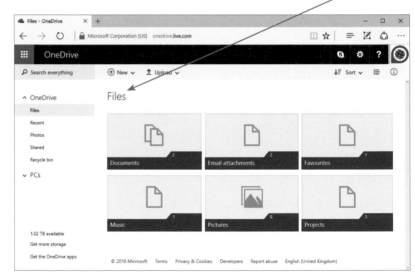

2 Open a folder and select an existing Word document – to see it open in "Reading" view within your browser

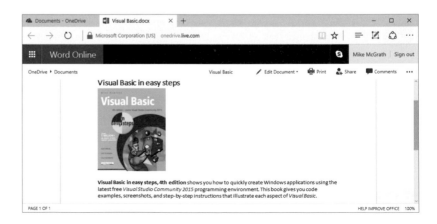

3 Click **Edit Document**, and then select **Edit in Word Online** – to see the document switch to "Editing" view within the browser

You can select **Edit Document**, **Edit in Word** to open the document immediately in Word on your device.

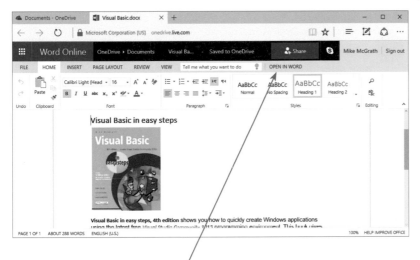

4 You can select **OPEN IN WORD** if you have Word installed on your device and require more than the limited functionality that Word Online provides

5 If you select an Excel spreadsheet from OneDrive, it will open directly in "Editing" view within the browser

When you opt to switch to an installed Office app you will receive a security warning. Unless you trust the file source, it is safer to continue editing with the Office Online app.

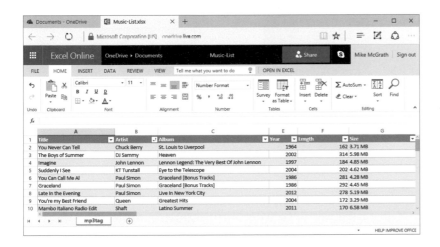

Office for Android

Microsoft has produced versions of Word, Excel, PowerPoint, Outlook and OneNote for Android devices. These are built from the ground up for touch gestures so are ideal to create and edit your Office documents from any location, on almost any device. Although optimized for Android, these apps all provide the familiar Office ribbon – so you feel instantly at home:

1 On your Android device, go to the Google Play Store and search for "microsoft office" to see the available apps

2 Tap the app you want to install, such as the **Microsoft Word** app

3 When the installation process is complete, tap the Word icon on your Home screen to launch the app

4 An initial screen lets you select one of the templates if you want to create a new document, or lets you open an existing document on your Android device

5 Tap the **Sign In** button and enter your Microsoft Account details to access your existing documents on OneDrive

6 A familiar Backstage screen now appears, where you can choose a location, a folder, and a file to open

You are not limited to OneDrive – choose **Add a place** for alternatives.

7 A copy of the file downloads to your Android device

8 The document then opens in the Word app for viewing, or editing with a limited selection of tools

For viewing only, select the **View** tab, then choose the 📖 **Read** icon to see the document neatly paginated for your device and its orientation.

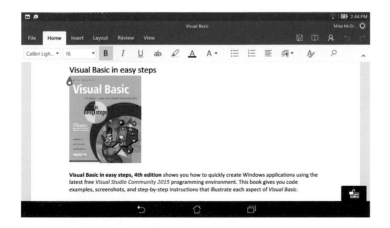

9 Tap **File**, then **Save**, to see any changes to the document get uploaded to OneDrive and applied to the file there

Sway Storytelling

Some editions of Office 2016 include the "Sway" digital storytelling application, which enables you to quickly create online presentations using pre-created content. Unlike the PowerPoint app, where you control all design aspects of the presentation, the Sway app makes many of the design decisions for you, to ensure your presentation looks great on any device.

Each Sway storyline comprises a series of content **Cards**.

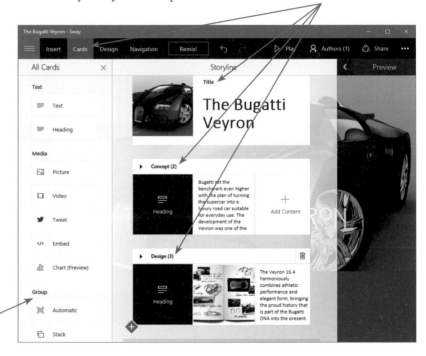

Hot tip

You can also arrange the Sway cards into Groups, for layout or comparison.

Beware

Remember that images you find online may be subject to copyright.

The basic content you place on a Sway card can simply be text you type in, or copy and paste, to create headings and narrative.

Additionally, you can place a whole variety of media content on a Sway card to illustrate your story with pictures, video and graphics.

The **Insert** button provides automatic context-based suggestions and offers you a host of sources from which you can easily import content into your Sway story.

When you have finished adding content to all the cards in your Sway story, you can use the **Design** button to suggest a general appearance for colors, backgrounds and fonts. You don't need to specify each aspect of the design, just choose a general preference and Sway will take care of the details for you.

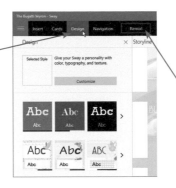

If you don't like the first appearance Sway creates, click **Remix** to see an alternative design.

You can also choose whether you prefer the story to be displayed horizontally or vertically using the **Navigation** button.

Click the **Play** button at any time to see how your Sway story will look.

Sway is not intended to be a replacement for PowerPoint, but provides an alternative way to quickly present ideas in a story. Sway is distinguished from PowerPoint by some key differences:

	Sway	**PowerPoint**
Content Source	Web	On device
Design	Minimal control	Full control
Delivery	Adapts to device	Screen slides
Location	Microsoft Sway servers	Corporate server or local computer

You need to be online to view a Sway presentation – it cannot be bundled into a portable file.

Visio Diagrams

There are some applications that are part of Office 2016, but are not included in any of the Office editions. The most popular of these is the "Visio" diagramming application, available as a standalone product or as an addition to an Office 365 subscription.

Visio is a vector drawing app that helps you easily visualize and communicate complex information. When you launch Visio it presents a wide range of templates to choose from, including business process flowcharts, network diagrams, workflow diagrams, database models, and software diagrams:

You can use **Search for online templates** if you don't see a template here that fits your needs.

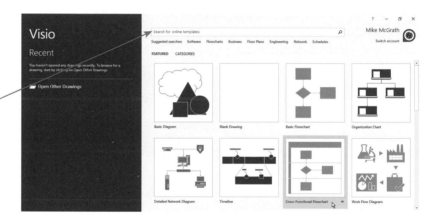

Select **Miscellaneous Flowchart Shapes** to see many more shapes to choose from.

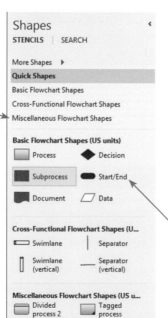

For any chosen template, Visio provides a series of appropriate "shapes" that you can drag onto a drawing area to build your diagram.

When you want to build a flowchart (probably the most common Visio diagram requirement) the shapes represent individual steps of a procedure, and can be labeled to describe the steps they represent.

The three fundamental basic shapes required to graphically illustrate a procedure in a flowchart are **Start/End**, **Process**, and **Decision** shapes. Other shapes, such as **Subprocess**, can be added to illustrate smaller steps.

...cont'd

The shapes added to a flowchart must be connected in a logical order to illustrate how the procedure progresses, from start to end. Connections can be made by first selecting the Visio **Home** tab, and then clicking the **Connector** button in the Tools group.

With the **Connector** selected, you can choose any shape then move the cursor to a subsequent shape to draw a connection. Alternatively, with the regular **Pointer Tool** selected, you can hover over a shape, then choose a subsequent shape to add and automatically connect from a context menu that appears.

Steps in a flowchart can be positioned within a "Swimlane" to further define individual stages of a procedure. For example, each defining a department through which the procedure must pass. Finally, you can select from a variety of themes, styles and colors, then save the diagram as a Microsoft Visio Drawing (**.vsdx**) file.

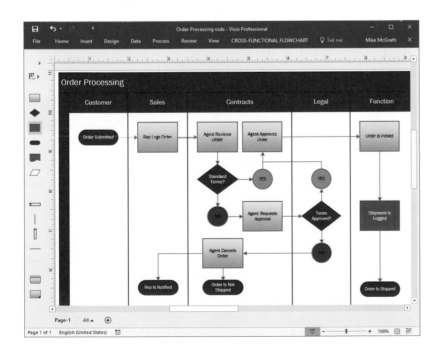

Hot tip

Double-click on a shape to add text.

Don't forget

You can import a Visio diagram into other Office apps, such as Word, or save it in a variety of other formats, such as **PDF**, **JPG**, and **HTML**.

Project Management

Another popular application that is not part of the core Office 2016 line-up is the "Project" planning application – available as a standalone product, or an addition to an Office 365 subscription.

Project is a management app that helps you easily visualize and plan projects from start to finish. When you launch Project it presents a wide range of templates to choose from, including software development, construction, business plan, marketing campaign, home move, wedding planner and product launch:

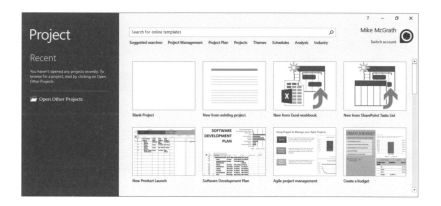

For any chosen template, Project presents a "Gantt chart", in which you can specify phases of your project and tasks within every phase. Each of these can be given a start date and duration to provide an overall picture of your project.

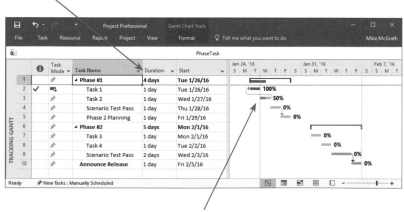

Hot tip

Gantt charts were originally developed by Henry Laurence Gantt (1861-1919) and used on major infrastructure projects, such as the Hoover dam and Interstate highway construction projects.

As the project proceeds, the % completion of each phase and task can be recorded to track the project's progress.

The tasks added to a Project Gantt chart can be linked to define logical task dependencies, where one task cannot start until another has finished. For example, a product testing task cannot begin until the task of manufacturing that product is completed. Project will automatically identify potential task scheduling problems and mark them with a red wavy underline.

Project will not allow you to move a task to a start date before a linked task ends, to prevent scheduling errors.

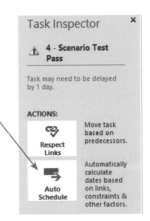

Task 2	1 day	Wed 1/27/16	Wed 1/27/16	?	Fix in Task Inspector...
Scenario Test Pass	0 days	Tue 1/26/16	Tue 1/26/16		Respect Links
Phase 2 Planning	1 day	Fri 1/29/16	Fri 1/29/16		Ignore Problems for This Task

Helpfully, the Project context menu offers an option to **Fix in Task Inspector** for any problems it identifies. Selecting the suggested action for **Auto Schedule** will automatically reschedule your project tasks to resolve the problem.

Project allows you to assign resources to each task and allocate unit costs for each resource. In this way, the application can multiply the scheduled time by the resource cost to produce a project budget.

Project provides lots of different chart views to monitor tasks, resources, team and costs.

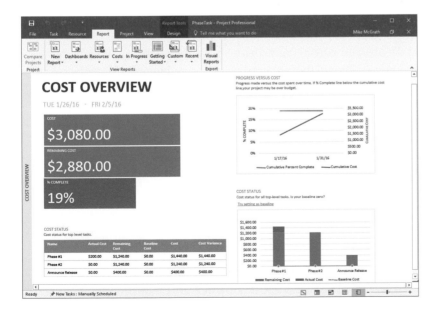

Business Products

Microsoft offers an additional range of high-end Office-related products specifically designed for business customers:

Microsoft Exchange
A hosted messaging solution that gives users access to email, calendar, contacts, and tasks from PCs, the web, and mobile devices. It enables administrators to use group policies and other administration tools, to manage the Exchange environment.

SharePoint Online
A collaboration platform for customized web services that include shared calendars, blogs, wikis, surveys, document libraries, shared task lists, and a community forum with search capabilities.

OneDrive for Business
A personal online storage space in the cloud, provided by the employee's company, which can be accessed from multiple devices. Used to store work files that can be shared with business colleagues, and edited together in real-time with Office Online.

Skype for Business
A hosted communications service that connects people anytime and from virtually anywhere. It gives users access to Presence, instant messaging, audio and video calling, online meetings, and extensive web conferencing capabilities.

Yammer
A secure and private enterprise social network. It allows employees to collaborate easily, and organize around projects so they can make decisions faster.

Power BI
An analytics service for sharing, managing, and consuming data queries and Excel workbooks that contain data queries, data models and reports. It connects users to a broad range of live data through easy-to-use dashboards, and provides interactive reports.

Compare Office 2016 products at **products. office.com/en-us/buy/ compare-microsoft- office-products**

Microsoft Dynamics CRM
A customer relationship management (CRM) solution that includes modules for sales force automation, marketing automation, and customer service and support. It is hosted in security-enhanced data centers owned and managed by Microsoft, backed by a 99.9 percent uptime service level agreement.

Index

Q

R

S

T

U